Landscape Architecture

AN INTRODUCTION

Published in 2014 by
Laurence King Publishing Ltd
361–373 City Road
London EC1V 1LR
United Kingdom
email: enquiries@laurenceking.com
www.laurenceking.com

A catalogue record for this book is available from the British Library.

ISBN: 978 1 78067 270 0

Design: Michael Lenz, Draught Associates
Senior editor: Peter Jones

Printed in China

Landscape Architecture

AN INTRODUCTION

Robert Holden & Jamie Liversedge

Contents

5. From Design Team to Long-term Landscape Management

6. Education and Employment

7. The Future

Introduction

Parc Citroën Cévennes, Paris

Few lay people really understand what landscape architecture actually is: something to do with planting schemes, or with laying out the space between buildings? Certainly both of those activities are involved, but the landscape architecture profession is much broader than that. This book aims to give a comprehensive overview of what landscape architecture is and some idea of how it may develop over the next 40 or 50 years. It is addressed in particular to those currently considering entering it as a profession.

A

Put simply, landscape architects plan, design and manage the landscape. Landscape architecture is an aesthetically based profession founded on an understanding of the landscape. That understanding requires knowledge of the land sciences, geology, soils, hydrology, botany, horticulture and ecology, and also of biology, chemistry and physics.

Landscape architecture grew out of garden design, and indeed landscape architecture and garden design continue to be linked. The critical difference between the two is that gardens tend to be enclosed and to be designed for the private individual, whereas landscape architecture is concerned with open space, the public realm, and the relationship between mankind's development activities and the natural environment. Landscape architecture is concerned with the public good, with community values and with human development and its impact on the land. The scale of landscape planning may be regional or even national: landscape architects can design whole new agricultural landscapes and forests. Landscape embraces the townscape and hence landscape architecture is also concerned with urban design. While its origins are in design, certain forms of landscape architecture practice are planning and management based. In some areas such as parks and gardens there can be an overlap between garden design and landscape architecture. Both of the authors of this book, for instance, are landscape architects who have designed private gardens. Both, however, have also been involved in large-scale planning projects, have undertaken environmental assessment work and have worked on urban design projects. If landscape architecture grew out of landscape gardening and was primarily a matter of aesthetics in the nineteenth century, in the twentieth century it became more ecologically focused. In the twenty-first century it has developed again, to become increasingly concerned with sustainability. It now deals with issues such as climate change and biodiversity – while, of course, continuing to address visual matters. It is an applied art based on scientific understanding.

B

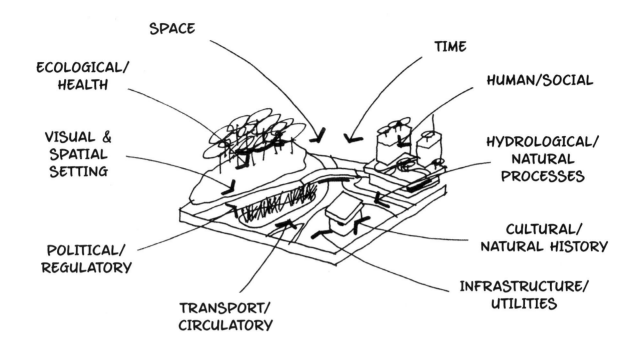

SPACE

TIME

ECOLOGICAL/
HEALTH

HUMAN/SOCIAL

VISUAL &
SPATIAL
SETTING

HYDROLOGICAL/
NATURAL
PROCESSES

CULTURAL/
NATURAL HISTORY

POLITICAL/
REGULATORY

INFRASTRUCTURE/
UTILITIES

TRANSPORT/
CIRCULATORY

Landscape architecture dealing with
the public realm:
A. The High Line, New York.
B. The South Bank, London.

Garden design applied to a private development:
C. Aphrodite Hills resort, Cyprus.

Landscape architects' clients are usually community (e.g. central and local government, charities) or corporate (e.g. developers). The classic landscape architecture practice is a private consultancy, consisting of either a single person or a larger team. But landscape architects may also work in multidisciplinary architectural, planning, engineering and urban design consultancies, or for quarrying and forestry companies. Many are likewise employed directly on a salaried basis by central and local government or by charitable foundations such as the National Trust or Groundwork Trust in Britain.

Landscape architects are unlikely to become rich. They tend to be less well paid than other development professionals such as architects, engineers and surveyors, though this situation has begun to change in many countries. In the UK, the Landscape Institute reported that the average salary for chartered landscape architects in 2012 was £41,055 while in the US the Department of Labor figures for 2010 reported a median annual salary of $62,090 (about the same as in the UK). Both figures are above the national average, but landscape architecture is not a highly paid profession.

Thanks to television, some chefs and garden designers enjoy high public profiles. This is not the case with landscape architects. Nonetheless, despite the often large amounts of administrative work involved, it can still be a highly rewarding pursuit. After all, this is a profession that deals with crucial environmental concerns. Sixty per cent of most towns and cities consist of streets, yards, gardens and parks, which together form 'open space' – the province of the landscape architect. All of the land we live on is the concern of landscape architects.

Landscape architecture deals with a very wide range of projects.

A. Parc Citroën Cévennes, Paris: town park on old industrial site.
B. Almas Tower, Dubai: Middle-Eastern city design.
C. Tower Place, London: urban spaces in commercial development.
D. London 2012 Olympic Park: derelict land reclamation, major world event and leading to long-term legacy.
E. Zoetermeer Floriade 1992, the Netherlands: international exposition.
F. Parc Diderot, Paris: urban neighbourhood park.
G. Barge Gardens, London: affordable, sustainable urban housing.
H. The Grand Axe, Paris: city planning.
I. Highcross Quarter, Leicester, UK: urban design.
J. Venlo Floriade 2012, the Netherlands: international exposition.

A landscape architect needs a technical understanding of construction and a thorough knowledge of plants.

A. Westergasfabriek, Amsterdam: native wetland planting.
B. More London: rills and use of Kilkenny Blue Limestone laid flexibly.
C. Painshill Park, Surrey, UK: conserved with plants available in the 1740s and '50s.
D. Chavasse Park, Liverpool One development, Liverpool, UK: immediate effect planting for commercial city centre shopping and open space development.
E. Dresden, Gorbitz-Kräutersiedlung, Germany: swales and sustainable drainage for refitted, system-built housing estate.
F. The Bur Juman Centre, Dubai: interior planting.
G. Rue Faidherbe, Lille: road construction detailing and street furniture design.

What is a landscape architect?

The work of a landscape architect is twofold: it involves work outside, where you have to relate to lots of different sorts of people; but it can also often involve lots of work in an office, maybe spending hours or days at a time in front of a computer screen. To work successfully as a landscape architect, you need:

- to be able to design and therefore to draw;
- to be able to write and present a case for conserving what is good in an existing site while proposing changes;
- to be able to work with people, and to communicate ideas;
- a technical understanding of construction, of building materials and how to use and assemble them, and therefore a reasonable comprehension of chemistry and physics as well as of building industry procedures;
- a thorough knowledge of plants and how to cultivate and manage them;
- an understanding of geology, soils and geomorphology, or how the land is formed, and of human, plant and animal ecology;
- patience; Geoffrey Jellicoe began work on the Hope Cement Works and Quarry, Derbyshire, UK, in 1940 and continued advising on it until the 1990s; landscape projects can take a long time, often years and even decades;
- financial acumen. You are charged with spending other people's money and must do so responsibly and accountably. You need to be able to administer, keep records, and take part in and often to chair meetings.

The word landscape – often spelled 'landskip' or 'lantskip' – became current in English in the seventeenth century. It comes from the Dutch *landschap* and was originally a painter's term, meaning 'a picture representing inland scenery as distinct from a seascape'. Soon it also came to encompass 'a background of scenery in a portrait' and then 'a prospect of inland scenery' and then 'a bird's-eye view' (from 1723). Today a principal meaning of landscape is 'an extensive area of land regarded as being visually distinct' (*The American Heritage Dictionary of the English Language*). According to the European Landscape Convention's definition: '"Landscape" means an area, as perceived by people, whose character is the result of the action and interaction of natural and/or human factors.' In short, landscape means land as seen or perceived.

A. Elegant structural design of precast concrete steps.
B. The Paris office of D. Paysage is typical of many medium-sized landscape architecture offices (ateliers in French, which sounds less corporate and indicates the creative design ambition of the French profession).

A

B

A thorough understanding of ecology, horticulture and the use of plants appropriate to place are fundamental to landscape architecture.

A. Liverpool One development, Liverpool, UK: use of grasses.
B. Hotel Riu Garopa, Sal, Cape Verde: palm trees.
C. Le Jardin des Géants, Lille, France: large grasses in a public park.
D. More London: use of monospecific block planting and box hedges.
E. Venlo Floriade 2012, the Netherlands: herbaceous flower display.
F. Thijsse Park, Amstelveen, the Netherlands: a controlled educational display using native peat bog plants.
G. Kench Villa Garden, Aphrodite Hills, Cyprus: Mediterranean plants.
H. The Mehdi Garden, Hadlow College, Kent, UK: use of large grasses and autumn colour display.
I. Barcelona Botanic Gardens, Spain: Mediterranean climatic zone plants.

Landscape architecture is about site: without a *locus* (Latin for 'place'), landscape architecture has no *raison d'être*. The classical idea of the *genius loci*, or presiding guardian or spirit of a place, is still central to the practice of landscape design. A landscape architect should be able to 'read' the landscape and understand the cultural forces that have influenced its formation. The story of civilization has been one of exploiting the land: forests have been cleared to create arable farmland and pasture, minerals have been mined, and existing land ownership patterns have been reorganized for economic, social and political reasons. The land is a document of such developments.

The metaphor of the palimpsest can be useful in explaining how to read a landscape. A palimpsest was a piece of goat's hide on which medieval scribes wrote. When they needed to reuse the valuable skin, they would scrape away the original text with a knife before writing over the traces. As a result, a palimpsest would come to hold traces of earlier layers of writing. This is comparable to the way many landscapes have developed. A landscape may contain the lines of Roman roads crossing prehistoric drovers' routes and Celtic field systems; remains of medieval fishponds have become ornamental lakes.

Definitions of landscape architecture include the art, science and management of landscape. The International Federation of Landscape Architects (IFLA) definition of 2003 has been lodged with the International Labour Organization as a proposed entry in its International Standard Classification of Occupations and reads: 'Landscape Architects conduct research and advise on planning, design and management of the outdoor environment and spaces, both within and beyond the built environment, and its conservation and sustainability of development.'

Given that landscape architecture originated in the United States, one should also look to the description offered by the American Society of Landscape Architects (ASLA), which was founded in 1899: 'Landscape Architecture encompasses the analysis, planning, design, management, and stewardship of the natural and built environment.' Stewardship is specified in addition to management since it suggests a more comprehensive approach, and analysis has been added to the IFLA's trio of planning, design and management. This is significant in terms of the growth of landscape character assessment in the past 20 years.

LANDSCAPE ARCHITECTURE IS A TRINITY OF DESIGN, PLANNING AND MANAGEMENT.

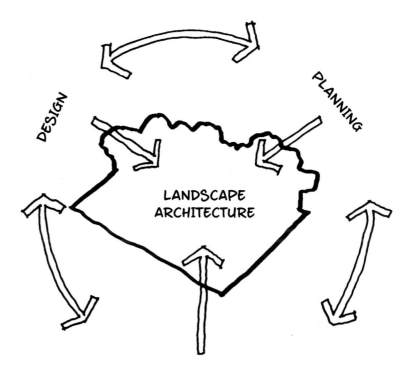

Finally, one should also look at the definition offered by the oldest professional body in Europe, Germany's *Bund Deutscher Landschaftsarchitekten* (BDLA), founded in 1913. 'Landscape design expresses the spirit of the time; it is a cultural language and involves both the conservation and reinterpretation of landscapes. Landscape architects combine ecological awareness and expertise with planning competence; they assess and prove the feasibility of plans and realize projects. They take creative responsibility for our natural reserves and for the interplay of the environment with our social and built environment.' The significant point about the BDLA definition is that it refers to landscape as a cultural construct ('a cultural language') and includes an ecological awareness. It also emphasizes the executive nature of the profession: landscape architects 'realize projects'. This is also explicit in the use of the word 'architect' in the BDLA's own name. But note that the nature of landscape architecture varies from country to country and from landscape to landscape. In the UK, the Landscape Institute's inclusion of landscape management and science memberships is atypical. In most other countries, landscape architects' professional associations emphasize design and planning. Nature conservationists may also be included in their number. In some countries the term 'landscape architect' is little used: in Russia, for instance, landscape architects often graduate in green engineering while in France and Spain landscape architects are not allowed to use the professionally protected word 'architect' in their titles and so call themselves *paysagistes or paisajistas* instead. In Germany, landscape planning is very important and many government landscape architects are planners. In the UK, the distinct profession of town planning is well established so there are far fewer landscape architects engaged in town and country planning than there are, say, in Germany. In the US, landscape architects often undertake plot layouts for housing estates or the design of road layouts; in some other countries, these tasks would be undertaken by surveyors or civil engineers.

A. Thijsse Park, Amstelveen, the Netherlands, demonstrates an ecological awareness and represents peatland habitat.

How this book is structured

Chapter 1 begins with an introduction to the scope of landscape architecture, looking at its origins and historical development, and then focuses on how it relates to political and economic forces. Afterwards we look at the aesthetic and environmental concerns that landscape architecture addresses and outline some of the ideas of ecology and sustainability that have influenced landscape architecture in the past half-century.

In chapter 2, we then look at pre-design work, discuss the definition of the brief, and review the sorts of clients landscape architects can work for. We briefly discuss costs and distinguish capital costs and management and maintenance costs and the revenue needed to pay for management. This leads to a discussion about fees. Finally, as part of pre-design work we look at site survey. Knowledge of site is fundamental to the development of the brief; it is also fundamental to landscape architecture.

In chapter 3, there is a description of design and of the design process and its basic elements, such as the significance of site, of inspiration, hierarchy and human scale, linearity, colour, form and texture, and human flow, and ideas of process and change.

Following this, in chapter 4, we discuss different techniques of presenting designs such as manual drawing and digital design, modelling and use of film and video, and mapping and Building Information Modelling, Geographic Information Systems, Zones of Theoretical Visibility and report writing and public presentations.

Project coordination and implementation are discussed in chapter 5, focusing on the nature of the design team and introducing the economics of parks and also long-term management. Here we go into the capital costs of landscape projects in some detail.

How to become a landscape architect is covered in chapter 6. This includes applying for a university course, obtaining work experience during education (internship), getting a job and thoughts on setting up your own practice.

Finally, in chapter 7, we end with a look at future opportunities and roles for landscape architects.

Thoughout the book case studies are used to illustrate and give meaning to, and provide context for, the main points in the text.

B. Landscape architecture is a wide-ranging profession that is often at the centre of placemaking. 9/11 Plaza water feature, New York, designed by Michael Arad and Peter Walker.

1
The History of Landscape Architecture: Changing Practices and Concerns

Stowe Gardens, Buckinghamshire, UK. The most famous eighteenth-century landscape garden in England. The designers were Charles Bridgeman and William Kent.

The histories of gardens, parks, agriculture and urban settlement are important to the practice of landscape architecture and design in the present. Like most art forms, landscape architecture is in constant dialogue with its past and its origins. To be a good landscape architect, it's therefore essential to know about the discipline's development across the centuries and changing emphases in professional practice. The focus is on the history of the landscape architecture profession. History permits us to see our place in the flow of time, and even to catch a glimpse of the future. For sure, the future is one of change. This chapter is designed to serve as an introduction to all of these areas.

Beginnings

Gardening is an ancient activity, which began as soon as man started living in towns. The cultivation of plants was the major step in mankind's move from nomadic hunting and cattle herding to agricultural settlement, which involved people living together in larger groups.

Garden design is both a popular activity and an aspect of aristocratic and leisured wealth. Mesopotamian culture developed the idea of the park, which was to give rise in the Middle Ages to both the hunting ground and the royal park and later, in the nineteenth century, to the public municipal park. Egyptian and Roman civilizations also fostered parks and gardens. In towns, the latter were courtyards enclosed by houses; in the countryside they became a series of enclosed spaces usually organized as outdoor rooms.

In East Asia, the first gardens that we know of developed in China, perhaps with the Shang dynasty (c. 1700–1046 BC) and certainly by the time of the Qin dynasty in 221 BC. The earliest imperial garden is said to have been the Shanglin garden built by the emperor Qin Shi Huang at Xianyang. As in the West, so in China, there were hunting parks, royal gardens and also merchants' and mandarins' gardens known as 'literati' gardens. Japanese gardens, which ultimately achieved a huge level of sophistication developed later from the first millennium AD on and were much influenced by Chinese examples. The Japanese also had palace, private and temple gardens.

Each civilization influences and shapes the landscape.

A. Fishbourne Roman Palace Gardens, Sussex, England.
B. Model of the first-century AD Fishbourne Roman Palace; the layout illustrates Roman symmetry.
C. The Acropolis, Athens, Greece: Athenian asymmetry.
D. The Nasrid Palaces, Alhambra Palace, Granada, Spain: with commanding site and enclosed courtyards and gardens integrated.

A

B

C

D

A

A. The castle garden: medieval castle gardens contained small plots and flowery meads: this manuscript illustration of the *Garden of Pleasure* shows a lutenist playing, the plots, the flowery mead or meadow, an elaborate fountain and a rill, the borders marked by a lattice edge and fruit trees.
B. Château de Villandry, Loire, France, a 1920s idealization of a Renaissance garden.

Given the profession's North American and European origins in nineteenth-century industrialized cities, it is worth looking at how historic example has influenced contemporary landscape architectural practice at various times. Chinese gardens included the idea of the borrowed landscape or view of the wider world as part of the composed pictures they offered. The medieval European garden explored the romance of the *pleasaunce* – a walled flower garden for pleasure – as a retreat.

The Renaissance garden was about creating an ideal model of nature (extensive, formal and in perfect symmetry) in relation to the revival of classical learning: hence primers on gardening began first with a section on geometry and then with a discussion of Roman gods and goddesses. The eighteenth-century English landscape garden revived the ideas of classical Rome, based on what people had seen when they went on the Grand Tour in

Italy. Ideas derived from Chinese gardens such as *sharawaggi* or studied irregularity also influenced the English landscape garden indirectly, just as idealizations of what Roman gardens might have been like had an impact on early eighteenth-century landscape gardeners. Later in the eighteenth century Indian garden motifs were introduced to the West.

All of this activity was accompanied by new horticultural discoveries and enthusiasms fed by plant collectors as Europeans explored the Americas and Africa, India, China and the Pacific. In the eighteenth and nineteenth centuries Russian gardeners and botanists explored further and further eastwards into Siberia and the Himalayas. Plants also migrated from Europe to other continents as colonists attempted to remake new lands in the image of their old ones. Centres of botanical study and horticulture such as Kew Gardens, on the outskirts of London, acted as botanical clearing houses. For example,

the rubber tree spread from Brazil to Malaysia via Kew Gardens and Indian tea plants were transplanted to be grown in East Africa.

While landscape gardening and garden design have a long history, landscape architecture is a relatively recent profession. It is also a profession with great promise for the future.

The growth of landscape architecture as a profession

The precursors of landscape architects in the nineteenth century were landscape gardeners such as Humphry Repton and Joseph Paxton in England and Andrew Jackson Downing in North America, who laid out private gardens and estates and then, with the growth of the cities, began to work on public parks. The scope of the discipline has since grown from a visual appreciation of the landscape to encompass the whole of mankind's physical relationship with the land. In a sense, this can be seen as a kind of democratization, moving out from private garden design to the wider man-made environment, for both the public and private good.

It was the American architect Calvert Vaux (1824–95) and the journalist, farmer and mine manager Frederick Law Olmsted (1822–1903) who in 1863 first applied the term 'landscape architecture' to their new profession. In 1858 they had won the competition to design Central Park in New York, and the Board of the Central Park Commission adopted their term in 1865. Olmsted and Vaux, first together and then separately, went on to design parks, campuses and housing estates in several cities in the 1860s and '70s.

With the growth of the North American city came large municipal park systems. For instance, in 1881 Olmsted and his nephew, John Charles Olmsted, began an 11km-long park system for Boston, linking Boston Common and the Charles River to Franklin Park on the edge of the city, which became known as the Emerald Necklace.

In Europe municipal park design was pursued by the likes of the landscape gardener Peter Josef Lenné (1789–1866), who designed the first public park in Germany, Park Klosterberg in Magdeburg (from the 1820s), the horticulturist Joseph Paxton (1803–65) in the 1850s in England (Olmsted visited Paxton's Birkenhead Park), and the engineer Jean-Charles Alphand (1817–91), who designed many Second Empire parks in Paris in the 1850s and '60s.

EMERALD NECKLACE – BOSTON

The Emerald Necklace is an 11km-long, chain of parks or linear park from central Boston extending westwards, and built in the 1880s to Frederick Law Olmsted's design, with detention basins to store stormwater drainage.

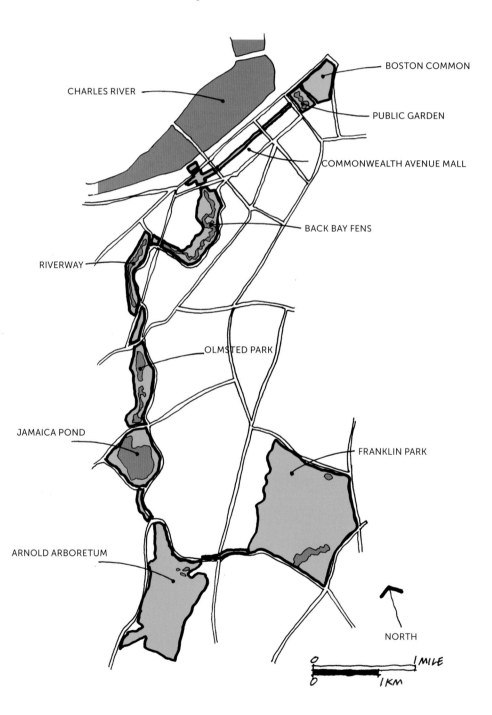

CHARLES RIVER

BOSTON COMMON

PUBLIC GARDEN

COMMONWEALTH AVENUE MALL

BACK BAY FENS

RIVERWAY

OLMSTED PARK

JAMAICA POND

FRANKLIN PARK

ARNOLD ARBORETUM

NORTH

0   1 MILE
0   1 KM

A. Looking north across Central Park to Harlem, New York. The park was design by Olmsted and Vaux.

B. Parc des Buttes Chaumont, Paris. The park was commissioned by the emperor Napoleon III and designed by Jean-Charles Alphand. One of the main features of the park, shown here, is the Belvedere of Sybil which sits on an exposed outcrop surrounded by a lake.

C. View across the lake to the Roman Boathouse at Birkenhead Park, Liverpool, UK, where Paxton shaped the land to create an undulating park for strolling, with pavilions, lakes, sequential gardens and rockeries.

In both North America and Europe, these designers were applying private park and garden design ideas to public projects and incorporating concepts regarding utility or public health in their layouts. The management of stormwater was key to Boston's Emerald Necklace, a series of parks with stormwater detention basins which stored run-off in times of heavy rain. While in Berlin, Paris and London air quality and ideas about the spread of disease by an atmospheric 'miasma' as well as concern about civil unrest (following the 1848 revolutions) impacted on designs.

In 1893 Olmsted was landscape architect for the Chicago Columbian World Exposition, which drew nearly 26 million visitors. Along with architect Daniel Hudson Burnham, Olmsted was central to the success of this first world exposition in the 'New World' which celebrated America's culture, civilization and international position. It was Olmsted who successfully argued for the location on Lake Michigan and designed the landscape and lakes of the 240-ha site.

On 4 January 1899, eleven landscape architects, including Downing Vaux, son of Calvert, met to form the American Society of Landscape Architects. In 1900 Harvard University opened its first landscape architecture course, with Frederick Law Olmsted Jr at its head. Further courses were established at Cornell in 1904, and at the Department of Forestry at Berkeley in 1913.

The North American model – of one or two practitioners promoting the practice and then, with like-minded professionals, establishing a professional association and starting an educational programme in landscape architecture – has been followed in other countries. The key impetus for the growth of the profession everywhere has been legislation requiring landscape plans and therefore the use of landscape architects. Political lobbying has been key to its development. In 1865, for instance, Olmsted served as one of the first Commissioners who managed the Congressional grant of the Yosemite Valley and the Mariposa Big Tree Grove to the State of California as a park. A century later in 1961 in Hong Kong, for example, it was statutory outline development legislation that led to the building of new towns with landscape masterplans in the 1960s and '70s and this required a landscape architecture profession to carry them out.

In the US, the establishment of the American National Park Service in 1916 led to the establishment of a landscape architecture division under Charles P. Punchard Jr. The Tennessee Valley Authority, set up in 1933, employed landscape architects in the design of new towns. Later in the same decade the New Deal policies of the Roosevelt administration included the work of the Farm Security Administration, for which landscape architects such as Garret Eckbo (1910–2000) planned new settlements in California for migrant farm workers from the Dust Bowl states of the Midwestern prairies. Eckbo, Daniel Kiley (1912–2004) and James C. Rose (1913–91) were classmates at Harvard in 1937–38, and together were responsible for the 'Harvard Revolution', applying the principles of Modernism to landscape architecture and emphasizing interlocking spaces, asymmetry, the importance of site, functionality, biomorphic shapes and the public good.

Parkways – landscaped roads for recreational driving, promoted by state and local governments – were widely constructed in the US in the 1930s and involved the input of landscape architects. An example is the Westchester County Park Commission's work, begun in 1932 with Gilmore D. Clarke as landscape architect. Such work was to influence *autobahn* (motorway) design in Germany in the 1930s and landscape architects played a significant part in their alignment, grading and planting.

A. Columbian World Exposition 1893, also known as The Chicago World's Fair, the exhibition attracted nearly 26 million visitors; Frederick Law Olmsted was landscape architect.
B. Bronx River Parkway in the 1920s. Built between 1907 and 1925, the US's first limited-access road with median strips and two carriageways.
C Farm Security Administration district landscape architects Vernon Demars, left, and Garret Eckbo, right, working on a site model of the Vallejo, California, defence housing dormitories in 1942, built to house workers in the expanding weapons industries of WWII. Eckbo went on to help found what later became Eckbo, Dean, Austin and Williams (EDAW), since part of the multi-disciplinary AECOM.

The growth of the profession in Europe

The first European professional landscape architecture association was the German *Bund Deutscher Landschaftsarchitekten* (BDLA), which began life in 1913 as the *Bund Deutscher Gartenarchitekten* (Federation of German Garden Architects). The profession expanded from this garden design basis in the 1920s and '30s. German *autobahn* landscape design was directed by Alwin Seifert (1890–1972) and there were 6,000 km by 1936.

Ideas concerning the value of public parks and gardens, the need for public access to sunshine and fresh air, etc. have traditionally been shared by political left and right. Landscape architects often need to become politically engaged in order to gain or generate commissions. Landscape and the environment fall under the remit of the public good or public benefit and so are often financed from the public purse.

Ideas about national plant communities were promoted by the Dutch naturalist Jacobus P. Thijsse (1865–1945) who had the idea of creating *heemparken* containing native landscape plant types to facilitate teaching about the flora of the Dutch countryside. This was an indication of the growing interest in natural plant communities and ecology in landscape architecture. The first *heempark* was the Thijseepark in Amstelveen, south of Amsterdam, from 1940s and the principles of the heemparken were to have a huge influence on landscape architecture in the next decades.

At the same time Moscow's 1930s *Genplan* celebrated the birch forests of Russia in the form of green wedges. These ideas of green wedges (or green corridors) and celebrating native woodland and landscape, were also expressed in an extreme form by German landscape architects after 1939 in their plans for 'Aryanizing' the conquered Polish landscape. The use of native species is still promoted, sometimes uncritically (because native sounds good) and sometimes because they serve as host plants for a large number of native insects and other wildlife. It should always be remembered that plants are part of a wider ecological community.

Erwin Barth (1880–1933) established the first university landscape architecture and garden design course in Germany in 1926, and in 1929 became the first holder of a chair in Garden Design at the Berlin Agriculture Technical School, later part of Friedrich-Wilhelm University, Berlin. His term ended with the coming of the Nazi regime in 1933. His successor was Heinrich Wiepking-Jürgensmann (1891–1973), who promoted nature conservation legislation. Ominously, he also worked for Himmler on landscape plans for the German colonization of Poland and Ukraine. Historically, landscape architecture has often been tied up with political imperatives. In the UK the practitioner who first really established the profession was Thomas Mawson (1861–1933). With Patrick Geddes (1854–1932), he used the term in the masterplan park design competition for Pittencrieff Park in Dunfermline in 1903. The Landscape Institute was established in 1929, with Mawson as its first president. Nonetheless, Mawson described himself as a 'garden architect' for much of his career.

A. Kröller-Müller Museum, near Arnhem, the Netherlands, with landscape and gardens originally designed by landscape and garden designer Mien Ruys in 1948.
B. Kröller-Müller Museum, sculpture designed by Professor Jan T.P. Bijhouwer and which opened in 1961 is a late Modernist design complementing the original 1938 museum of Henry Van der Velde.

The expansion of the profession worldwide

By the 1940s the discipline was established in North America and much of north-western Europe. Professional associations were set up in Japan in 1964, in Australia in 1966 and in New Zealand in 1969. More recently a Society of Landscape Architects has been established in both China (in 1989) and India (in 2003). By the twenty-first century landscape architecture was firmly established worldwide with the exception of Africa (outside of South Africa) and parts of the Middle East. Recently, the profession has grown most dynamically in China, where the expansion of the economy has led to large-scale environmental problems comparable to the challenges posed by industrialization in nineteenth- and twentieth-century Europe and North America. The Chinese state has responded by enacting environmental legislation that fosters the growth of the profession.

The International Federation of Landscape Architects (IFLA) was established in 1948, with Sir Geoffrey Jellicoe (1900–96) as its first president, while the European Federation for Landscape Architecture (EFLA) began its meetings in 1989 and now works with IFLA as its European Region, IFLA Europe.

C. Sha Tin Town Park, Hong Kong: the growth of new towns in the New Territories, first proposed in the 1960s to accommodate the growing population, led to the development of the landscape architecture profession from the late 1970s onwards.

C

Painshill Park, Surrey, UK

Historic landscape garden conservation

Painshill was a well-known landscape garden developed by Charles Hamilton from 1738 to 1773 at Chobham, south-west of London. The estate had been divided up in 1948 and much had been planted for forestry, the garden buildings were in ruins and the lake was overgrown.

Elmbridge Borough Council had been buying parcels of the Painshill Park estate, which had originally covered 100 hectares, since 1974. In April 1981, Janie Burford was appointed landscape architect and the Painshill Park Trust was formed. There was no staff and little money. But the study of material relating to the park began and work started on site using volunteers. Burford recalls:

'We needed to understand the mind of Charles Hamilton, the topography of the site and every element of his vision and design. He was an exceptionally strong designer, artist and plantsman, and very early on I realized that it was an enormous privilege to be walking in his footsteps and trying to re-create the genius of the man.'

Opening up the site and starting the project was possible through the government-funded Manpower Services Commission (MSC), which ran work-experience schemes for the long-term unemployed. Some of the team were graduates in the disciplines of archaeology, natural sciences, horticulture and landscape and there was a historian and archivist who used documentary evidence to help assemble the missing details of Painshill's development and layout.

Burford commissioned a survey of historic trees, so as to 'read' the history of the estate from tree dating. This was done by a team recruited through the MSC under the supervision of National Trust tree surveyor Johnny Phibbs. The survey recorded 169 trees surviving from Hamilton's time, including four Cedars of Lebanon. This was supplemented by archaeological evidence of the sites of buildings that had disappeared, like the Bath House and the Temple of Bacchus. Documentary sources were then cross-referenced with direct observational evidence in the tree records and the archaeology to build a complete picture.

This led to a masterplan to cover the restoration of the site and its development for public use. The first building to be restored was the Gothick Temple. The remains of the timber and plaster temple had been supported by scaffolding for more than ten years. One of the challenges was that many of the buildings had been built very cheaply because Hamilton was not wealthy and had built in timber and plaster to represent stone.

Burford was in effect 'a ranger, a plantswoman, an administrator, a landscape historian and a landscape architect all in one' but also a fundraiser. In the first 20 years of the formation of the Trust, £20 million was raised for the conservation project.

Ensuring public access to the site took ten years because of local opposition and access was finally secured by a new footbridge across the River Mole to the south-west of the site. These delays, however, gave the restoration time to develop and settle in and allowed the Trust time to develop an education strategy.

In 1994 the Painshill Park Trust received a Europa Nostra medal for 'the exemplary restoration, from a state of extreme neglect, of a most important eighteenth-century landscape park and its extraordinary garden buildings'.

Burford retired from Painshill at the end of 2003. However, she has since become a trustee of the Chiswick House and Gardens Trust, which with English Heritage and the London Borough of Hounslow is supervising the restoration of Lord Burlington's Chiswick House and gardens.

A

B

C

Painshill Park, Chobham, an English landscape garden resurrected.

A. The restored Chinese bridge.
B. Grotto walls and ceiling of calcite, fluorite and gypsum.
C. An eighteenth-century landscape garden won back from forestry planting in the 1940s. The grotto is to the right.

Planning

Historically, landscape planning has aimed to reconcile human development with the ecological, cultural and geographical features of the landscape. This has been done largely by the protection of specially valued areas. Until recently, its role was largely conservationist and limited. However, this has changed in the past half-century so that landscape planning has become much more proactive, mapping and promoting the whole landscape rather than just exclusive, already protected areas.

Illustrative of the conservationist or protectionist approach are the American National Parks. In the 1850s Galen Clark, a homesteader, was so impressed by the Giant Sequoia trees of Mariposa County, California, that he called for their protection from loggers. With support from photographer Carlton Watkins and US senator John Conness, this led to proposals to protect the whole of the Yosemite Valley. In 1864 (at the height of the Civil War) President Lincoln signed the Yosemite Grant to protect Yosemite Valley and the Mariposa Grove of Giant Sequoias. This was the first piece of federal land set aside by the US Congress for public use and preservation. Having spent three centuries in westward expansion, the North American colonists suddenly grasped that the wilderness was a valuable and threatened commodity. This was followed by further protectionist measures being enacted elsewhere: for instance, the Yellowstone National Park was set up by the US Congress in 1872. This was managed federally; eventually the whole system of US National Parks was rationalized with the formation of the US National Parks Service in 1916.

In Germany the term *Naturdenkmal* ('nature monument') was coined by the geographer Alexander von Humboldt in 1814 to refer to large or historically significant trees, and was later expanded to include geological and topographical features and whole landscapes. The botanist Hugo Conwentz was a follower of Humboldt and became the first director of the Prussian *Staatliche Stelle für Naturdenkmalpflege* (State Office for Nature Monument Protection), set up in Danzig in 1904. The nature conservation movement in the 1920s and '30s promoted *Landschaftspflege* – literally, 'landscape care' – which encouraged stewardship of the landscape. By the 1930s this involved a vision of the *Heimat* (homeland and community), which included an orderly and organized integration of new industry and transport.

Contemporary with the development of nature and landscape conservation in Germany in the early twentieth century, a non-state organization was set up in England in 1895, the National Trust, initially to purchase and protect wetlands like Wicken Fen in Cambridgeshire and mountains in the Lake District. In the 1930s there were large-scale protests about restrictions on access to upland moorland, such as the Kinder Scout mass trespass of 1932. Such events led to the 1949 National Park Act. The ten National Parks established in this way were very different from the wilderness areas represented by the US National Parks. US national parks are in the main wilderness areas, with few inhabitants, but in Britain there is little such wilderness; in Britain national parks included farms and settled areas: they conserve cultural (or human-influenced) landscapes.

A. Cadair Idris in the Snowdonia National
   Park, Wales: British National Parks contain
   farms and villages.
B. The Lüneburg Heath in North Germany was the
   first large German nature reserve to be formally
   protected by law in 1921 when an area of 234
   square kilometres was protected. Today 27 per
   cent of the land area in Germany has some form
   of nature and landscape protection status.
C. Yosemite National Park, a wilderness
   conserved for the nation.

Such developments were essentially protectionist and involved identifying areas of special interest and drawing lines on a map to protect them. Examples are European Special Areas of Conservation (SACs) and Special Protection Areas (SPAs), which form part of a European network known as 'Natura 2000', which applies to both bird sites and habitat sites. The situation has changed considerably over the last 20 years, so that the whole landscape now falls under the remit of landscape planning. For instance, Landscape Character Assessments cover the whole of a county or country, while the Council of Europe's European Landscape Convention of 2000 covers the whole landscape. As it says: 'this Convention applies to the entire territory of the Parties and covers natural, rural, urban and peri-urban areas. It includes land, inland water and marine areas. It concerns landscapes that might be considered outstanding as well as everyday or degraded landscapes.' The above moves to protect and value the landscape have often been led by nature conservationists, botanists, ecologists and those concerned with public access to the countryside. But landscape architects have usually been involved because, as a profession, they have some of the responsibility for carrying out such policies.

Landscape planning also involves the laying out of new landscapes. For example, in the Netherlands there was extensive land reclamation, and new polders were developed in the Zuider Zee between 1921 and 1975 following the plans of Cornelis Lely which were first devised in 1891. From 1921 to 2004 there was also extensive landscape consolidation (*ruijlverkaveling*) covering 1.4 million ha. This was similar to the earlier enclosure movement in England and involved the consolidation of fragmented agricultural plots and in effect the replanning of the whole countryside. Landscape architects worked on new polder landscapes (including one of the authors as a student) and on landscape consolidation.

In Germany, the Federal Nature Conservation Act of 1977 requires the preparation of landscape plans 'to protect, maintain, further develop and, if necessary, restore the visual diversity, uniqueness/distinctiveness and beauty of landscapes' working through federal, *Länder* and local councils producing regional landscape plans, local landscape plans and green structure plans. As a result of a century of nature conservation planning in Germany since the setting up of the Prussian State Office for Nature Monument Protection in 1904 there are now several categories of protected areas in Germany such as national parks, biosphere reserves, landscape protection areas, nature parks and Natura 2000 sites. The 2002 Federal Nature Conservation Act also enacted a new requirement for the *Länder* to set up networks of interlinked biotopes for at least 10 per cent of their land area. There have also been policies of active soil conservation as part of these general nature conservation and landscape planning policies.

A. The Douro Valley, Portugal.
B. Landscape-led Ile-de France Masterplan (Schéma Directeur de la Région Ile-de-France) Paris, France, which sets Paris in its greater landscape.
C. Cornwall Historic Landscape Character Zones. Map plotted in 1994.

A

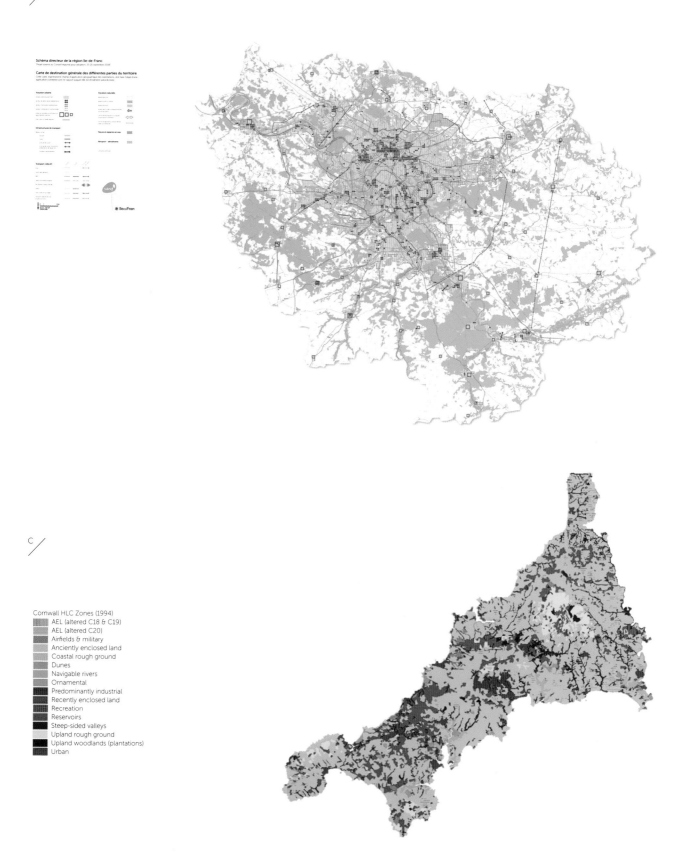

Schéma directeur de la région Île-de-Franc
Projet adopté au Conseil régional pour adoption 25-26 septembre 2008

Carte de destination générale des différentes parties du territoire
Cette carte, exprimant le champ d'application géographique des orientations, doit faire l'objet d'une
application combinée avec le rapport auquel elle est étroitement subordonnée.

C /

Cornwall HLC Zones (1994)
AEL (altered C18 & C19)
AEL (altered C20)
Airfields & military
Anciently enclosed land
Coastal rough ground
Dunes
Navigable rivers
Ornamental
Predominantly industrial
Recently enclosed land
Recreation
Reservoirs
Steep-sided valleys
Upland rough ground
Upland woodlands (plantations)
Urban

City planning and structural green space

London and Frankfurt are examples of cities where green belts have been developed. The Frankfurt *GrünGürtel* follows the ideas of the town planner Ernst May in the 1920s for residential developments with access to green space provided in the form of gardens established around the old city walls. The *GrünGürtel* was formally set up in 1991 and now comprises 8,000ha including forests, fields, meadows, gardens, parks, orchards, fields, streams and ponds. Frankfurt is a remarkable city in that green space comprises 50 per cent of the urban area.

The London Green Belt really began in 1935 when the London County Council began giving grants to surrounding county councils to buy land for conservation purposes and to put into effect ideas proposed by Sir Raymond Unwin in the 1920s. Concerns included a desire for breathing space in the face of population 'overspill' and the 'menace of the outward sprawl of building which leads to ribbon development, conurbation (the joining up of towns) and the engulfment of small towns'. Such thinking gave rise to the Green Belt Act of 1938, later reinforced by Patrick Abercrombie's Greater London Plan of 1944 and then the Town and Country Planning Act of 1947, which established a country-wide planning system including provision for green belts. There are now 14 green belts controlling development and protecting open land, usually farmland, around English cities from Oxford to the great conurbations of the Midlands such as Birmingham and North such as Liverpool, Manchester and Leeds.

The 1935 *Genplan* or General Plan for the reconstruction of Moscow set the model for green wedges or corridors penetrating the city. The latter are largely birch forest rather than the fields, farms and woodlands that typify the London Green Belt. The wedges worked well in Soviet times when most people travelled by public transport, providing accessible recreation areas within walking distance of the city's apartment blocks.

Similar ideas influenced the planners in Copenhagen, who developed the so-called Green Finger Plan in 1947. This used the five fingers of the main railway lines and roads as a structure for future development radiating from the 'palm' of the old nineteenth-century city. Green wedges in between the fingers were designed to provide land for agriculture and recreation, easily accessible from the adjacent housing. With the building of the road and railway bridge across the Øresund to Sweden, an extra finger was added to the south across the island of Amager. Planning in Copenhagen includes active policies to promote pedestrian and bicycle travel, with the result that 40 per cent of journeys to work in the Danish capital are made using bicycles. Copenhagen introduced its cycle hire scheme in 1995. In Copenhagen 36 per cent of all journeys are made by bicycle.

A. Housing, Jönköping, Sweden, from the 1940s, showing a landscape setting.
B. Port Sunlight, Merseyside, UK, from the 1890s an example of the Garden City ideal.

EXAMPLES OF GREEN BELT PLANNING

A

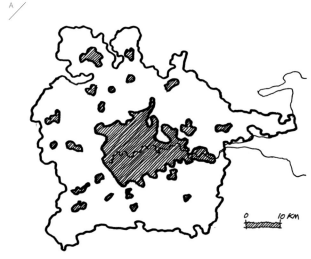

The London Green Belt.

B

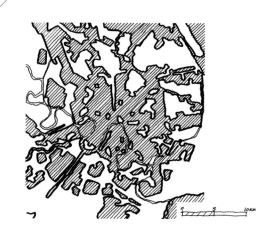

The Moscow *Genplan* of 1935 with wedges of birch forest.

C

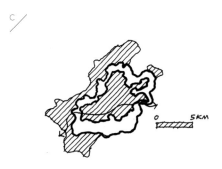

The Frankfurt *GrünGürtel*.

D

The Copenhagen 'Green Finger Plan'.

Changing styles: from Modernism to Postmodernism and beyond

For much of its history, landscape architecture has followed architectural and engineering design practice. In the mid-twentieth century landscape designers, like architects, donned white lab coats and tended to think of themselves as scientists, reordering cities and countryside according to a functional aesthetic that rejected the symmetrical but curiously adopted the asymmetric picturesque aesthetic of the eighteenth century as a model. Post-war English New Towns are often set in a landscape of mounds and tree clumps which is reminiscent of a Capability Brown park in miniature.

The reaction to this prescriptive 'scientific' approach in the 1970s was to adopt forms of community action that tried to engage the whole community. More recently, in some countries landscape architects have developed a more corporate approach and set up as limited companies. Some landscape consultancy practices have sold up to large professional services companies who also run insurance and pension schemes. Search for landscape architecture in the main company website and you see it listed in a bundle of professional consultancy services under 'property services'.

MODERNISM TO POSTMODERN AND BEYOND

The main artistic movement of the twentieth century to influence landscape architecture was Modernism, which might be defined as absolute, functionalist and orthogonal (meaning rectilinear) in character, and marked by an absence of ornament. Modernism's influence in landscape design can be seen particularly in the work of the 'Harvard Three', Garret Eckbo, Daniel Kiley and James C. Rose, from the late 1930s onwards, and in the public spaces created by Peter Shepheard and Peter Youngman for the 1951 Festival of Britain. The English New Towns of the early 1950s, Harlow, Crawley and Hemel Hempstead, were designed in a Scandinavian-influenced, English Modernism. While later English new towns such as Cumbernauld were more Brutalistic yet curiously the landscape design maintained a form of stripped-down picturesque style marked by the use of standard trees and flowing mounds.

Postmodernism, by contrast, is rich in surface ornament, non-rectilinearity and references to historical forms. Examples of some of these elements are found in the late historicist work of Geoffrey Jellicoe (who in the 1950s had been a strict Modernist) or, more recently, in the Canberra Garden of Australian Dreams of 2001 by Richard Weller and Vladimir Sitta of Room 4.1.3, which is full of symbolism.

Bet Figueras's Barcelona Botanic Gardens is structured by acute angular forms with zigzagging paths and uses Corten steel, both markers of landscape design of the turn of the twentieth century. It is certainly not Modernist, but its interest is as much in the creation of habitats based on the five worldwide Mediterranean climatic regions as in the sharp stylistic forms of the distorted net which is the plan.

A

A. The Stockholm Woodland Crematorium of 1940 is a masterpiece of Modernist architecture coupled with a picturesque landscape of mounds and trees. The designers were Erik Gunnar Asplund and Sigurd Lewerentz.
B. Barcelona Botanic Gardens, Spain with a built structure of acute, angular shapes draped over the hillside of Montjuïc.
C. Garden of Australian Dreams, Canberra: a symbolic and allegorical design.

LA VILLETTE TO LANDSCAPE URBANISM

Perhaps the most significant and influential design of the past thirty years is the Office of Metropolitan Architecture's entry for the Parc de La Villette competition in Paris in 1982–83. It won second prize and so wasn't actually built. Nonetheless, its parallel-stripe plan form has reverberated through the landscape design of the past few decades, as can be seen in Robert Townshend's linear urban design for the More London office development in London (1999–) or more recently Michel Corajoud's Cour du Maroc park in Paris (2005–7). Corajoud worked on the original La Villette design with OMA. The OMA La Villette design was avowedly more about programmatic ideas than a style.

It established arbitrary ways of structuring the park, such as contrasting strips each 50m wide, in turn subdivisible by 5m widths. The idea of sharp contrasts in a plan comes from Rem Koolhaas's student dissertation on the Berlin Wall. The aim was to establish an architectural structure for a programme which to quote OMA combines a 'programmatic instability with architectural specificity (which) will eventually generate a park'.

Post-industrial landscapes have been discussed in relation to landscape and urban design since the 1980s. Since this point there has been a fresh appreciation of the value of the products of industry and its cultural and historical importance together with the ecological value of the derelict sites which became vegetated naturally. In his account of his High Line urban park in New York (2003), landscape architect James Corner describes:

> 'the post-industrial railroad character of the site – the rail tracks, the linearity, and the fact that it really is a thin, narrow ribbon... The entire High Line really cuts through blocks and buildings, and I sought to create a distinct juxtaposition where there is this green ribbon existing against the stoic grid of the city... There is also this almost sad, melancholic, silence that permeates the place... We wanted to... give people the feeling that they've come across a secret, magic garden in the sky.'

In this statement, we can see suggestions of the Office of Metropolitan Architecture's Parc de La Villette design, which was about cutting and 'distinct juxtapositions', and post-industrial landscapes such as Latz + Partner's Duisburg Nord Landschaftspark of 1991 onwards, while the most obvious precedent for the functional design idea of the railway viaduct-made-park is the earlier Promenade Plantée (opened 1993) by Jacques Vergely in Paris (itself a historicist design). Yet it was James Corner who has particularly promoted the label of landscape urbanism, meaning the shaping of cities on the basis of landscape ideas as opposed to building-centred urbanism.

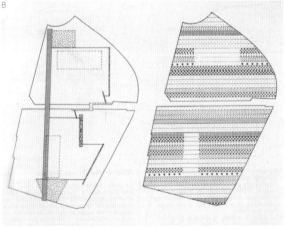

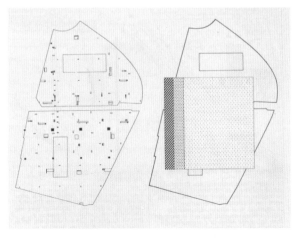

A. Jardin d'Eole, Paris, designed by Michel Corajoud using a stripes theme and influenced by the OMA La Villette competition entry of 20 years earlier.

B. Parc de La Villette competition, the OMA entry of 1982, with the stripes or horizontal bands designating different activities.

C. More London, London: the same parallel linearity is found in Robert Townshend's design designed 20 years after the 1982–83 La Villette competition.

D. The High Line, New York: the way up.

E. The High Line, New York: created on a disused railway viaduct.

F. The High Line, New York: it straddles the streets of Manhattan's West Side.

G. The High Line, New York: with gardens in the sky.

H. The High Line, New York: offering a refuge and a prospect.

A CAVEAT ABOUT STYLES

Perhaps the ultimate Postmodernist design is that for the River Manzanares, Madrid, by West 8. It is certainly not orthogonal, but it is playful and uses symbolism. However, ask the designer Adriaan Geuze and he will reject all stylistic labels. Design is not about application of a style, but rather is about development and application of ideas which will draw on contemporary design, ideas and concerns, which theorists and historians will categorize afterwards. Isms make convenient pigeonholes for design discussion.

A. Two *madrileños* by the cherry planters, River Manzanares, Madrid.
B. Avenida de Portugal, River Manzanares, Madrid. The urban motorway is placed in a tunnel and a park made above; part of the network of 43km of tunnels with public open space above.
C. Salón de Pinos and Oblique Bridge, River Manzanares, Madrid: West 8 have revealed the course of the river and provided riverside access.
D. Duisburg Nord Landschaftspark: view from the 65m-high blast furnaces.

E. Duisburg Nord Landschaftspark: bunkers made into play pens.
F. Duisburg Nord Landschaftspark: gardens in the bunkers.
G. Duisburg Nord Landschaftspark: water treatment and cleaning is key to the way Peter and Anne-Liese Latz have dealt with pollution.
H. Duisburg Nord Landschaftspark: former ore storage bunkers now house gardens.
I. Duisburg Nord Landschaftspark: under the blast furnaces of the old steelworks.

Emscher Park, Ruhr Valley, Germany

Environmental transformation of a city region

The section of the Ruhr between Duisburg and Essen was the most economically depressed area in the former West Germany. In the 1980s coal mines and steel mills were closing down with a significant impact on the population of 2.5 million people. By way of response, the Nordrhein-Westfalien Länder government set up the Emscher Park Internationale Bauausstellung (IBA), which ran from 1989 to 1999 and aimed to revitalize the economy of the whole area by underwriting environmental improvements. In other words, the state government saw an area that was suffering economic, social and environmental problems and devised a way forward that put ecology and environment first.

The thinking, in other words, was: fix the environment and the economy would improve. The scheme's principal aims included:

- the ecological regeneration of the 350km length of the River Emscher and its tributaries;
- the creation of the Emscher Landscape Park (300km^2 of parks and green spaces linked by cycle and footpath routes);
- the upgrading of 3,000 existing homes and the building of 3,000 new ones;
- job-creation schemes based on a chain of 22 technology centres set in new parkland;
- the finding of new uses for industrial buildings and landmarks.

Every individual project had to show a net ecological gain.

The scheme was government-led. Two-thirds of the total £1.13 billion funding came from federal, *Länder* and European Union sources; one-third came from the private sector. The IBA acted as a catalyst, operating through the 17 local authorities with a staff of just 30 people and a steering committee including representatives from local authorities, trade unions, and nature conservation and planning organizations.

The boldest project was the reclamation of the River Emscher, which in the nineteenth century had been sacrificed to carrying industrial waste and sewage. With the River Emscher effectively turned into an open sewer, seasonal flooding led to typhoid epidemics. As a result, in 1904 the *Emschergenossenschaft* (the Emscher water management association) was established by local councils and industrial concerns to stop flooding. This was done by building dykes and canalizing the Emscher and lining the tributaries with concrete.

The decline of coal mining and the ending of the consequent problem of subsidence permitted the removal of the concrete and dykes and the re-creation of the 350km network of rivers and tributaries as a natural river system with water meadows. Industrial effluent is now channelled into a piped sewerage system connecting to five new sewage plants. The whole river system is in the process of being renaturalized.

Linked to the regeneration of the river is the 300km^2 Emscher Landscape Park which has been designed as a green lung for the whole region, although further parkland and green spaces were created throughout the urban area. In total, the Emscher Park fostered 450 projects. Major individual projects included the

200ha Duisburg Nord Landschaftspark by Anna-Liese and Peter Latz, which reuses the A.G. Thyssen steelworks which had closed in 1985. The project is a major work of interpretation of industrial history: one can now climb the 65m-high blast furnace, while below mountaineering climbers practise rock climbing in old ore bunkers and heavy metal bands play from the slag heaps.

In total 13 major parks were created throughout the Ruhr. Elsewhere business and science parks have been developed such as the science park in Gelsenkirchen Rheinelbe or the 40ha Erin Business Park on the site of the former Erin coal mine in Castrop-Rauxel, opened in 1867 by Irishman William Thomas Mulvany. These represent just a few of the 71 employment-creation projects.

Although the IBA ended in 1999, the work continues through the local councils and two regional agencies.

A. The Emscher Park IBA (*Internationale Bauausstellung*) in the Ruhrgebiet, involved decanalising streams and restoring them as natural watercourses.

B. Example of canalized stream, with culvert, at the Duisburg Nord Landschaftspark.

C. The Erin Business Park (built on the site of an old coal mine) in Castrop-Rauxel is one of over 120 projects in the Emscher Park IBA, all providing a net ecological gain.

Changing priorities: ecology, biodiversity and sustainability

For the past half-century landscape architecture has been increasingly influenced by the science of ecology. Basic ecological definitions are now key to an understanding of the ways in which landscape architecture is developing. Ecological ideas have also fundamentally impacted on concerns for sustainability, which is a growing concern for landscape architects.

Ecology is the study of the natural environment and human, animal and plant communities and their interrelationships. The name has the same Greek stem, *oikos* (meaning 'house'), as economy and was first coined in 1866 by the German biologist Ernst Haeckel. Ecology looks at:

- life processes and adaptation;
- the distribution and abundance of organisms;
- the movement of energy and materials;
- ecosystem succession;
- biodiversity.

In most other countries, it is plant ecology that has had the greatest influence on landscape architects, particularly since the 1950s. Work by local botanists on native plant communities have been very influential. Ecology is by its nature holistic, in the sense that it regards the whole system as more than the sum of its individual parts. At its extreme (or most advanced), this has influenced biogeochemical theories such as the Gaia hypothesis formulated by the chemist and earth scientist James Lovelock in the 1970s, which proposes the whole planet to be a self-regulating and dynamic system.

A

B

Landscape architects have to understand the differences between habitat types.

A. Gunung Pulai Forest, Johor, Malaysia: a Virgin Jungle Reserve with *Dipterocarpus*, *Shorea*, and *Cleistanthus* trees.
B. Rotorua geothermal lakes, New Zealand with silicate and mineral formations.
C. Industrial wasteland, UK, with ruderal or spontaneous herbaceous pioneer vegetation.
D. Beech woodland, France.
E. Karst limestone landscape, Guilin, China, formed by water dissolving the rock along fractures or bedding planes in the limestone.
F. Saltwater marsh, Sussex, UK.
G. Insel Hombroich Wetlands, Germany.
H. Terraced rice fields, Japan.
I. Coastal maquis, Cyprus.

A

Habitats vary across the world.

A. Urban public realm, London.
B. Volcanic desert, Cape Verde Islands.
C. Upland reafforestation with spruce
    planted since 1919, Wales.
D. Sand dune protection, Ilha Deserta
    in the Parque Natural da Ria Formosa,
    Faro, Portugal.
E. Planted palms, public realm, Dubai.
F. Sinai Desert, Egypt.
G. Tree ferns, Taranaki, New Zealand.
H. Mountain pine forest, Greece.
I. Palm grasslands, Indonesia.

B

C

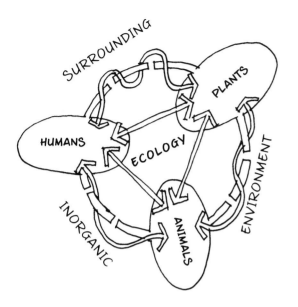

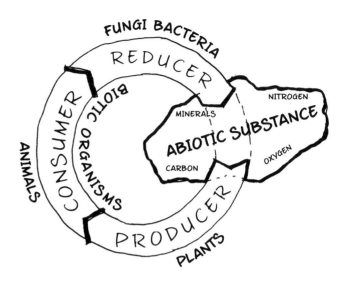

Ecosystems, which are the total environment, include all the living organisms and the inert or non-living physical aspects of that ecosystem such as air, soil, water and exposure to the sun. For example, a forest may be an ecosystem: a planted forest is a modified or human-made ecosystem. The living components of such a system are generally referred to as a community. So a pine forest may be a particular plant community, named for its dominant species.

At a much larger scale there are biomes, which are globally significant groups of ecosystems – the Mediterranean biome is one such. Habitat refers to the physical environment in which a community of ecosystems may develop, whether mountain-top alpine habitats, marshlands or chalk grasslands. A biotope is the habitat of a biological community: for instance, a tropical rainforest. A biotope may be artificial – for example, a roof garden can create a habitat for nesting birds. By contrast, a niche is the physical environment of a single species.

Natural resource management involves stewardship of the landscape. Important concepts include succession and biodiversity. Succession is the process by which a plant or animal community develops and changes into another community until a stable climax is reached – here climax refers to a long-lasting, stable community. For instance, former railway yards may become birch woodland, which then develops into ash and oak woodland as soil fertility develops.

The 1992 United Nations Convention on Biological Diversity defines biodiversity as 'the variability among living organisms from all sources including, *inter alia*, terrestrial, marine and other aquatic ecosystems and the ecological complexes of which they are part; this includes diversity within species, between species and of ecosystems'. We have introduced the United Nations definition here to underline the point again that there is a political imperative in environmental science. But phrases and words are often used without a full understanding of their meaning, so it is important that landscape architects understand the science behind these very live political agendas. We return to this theme in our final chapter.

A

A. Managed chestnut coppice with bluebell understorey.
B. Hoge Veluwe National Park, near Arnhem, the Netherlands: heathland being restored from early twentieth-century forestry.
C. Hoge Veluwe National Park: restoration of inland sand dunes.
D. Hoge Veluwe National Park: early twentieth-century forestry in the background.
E. Insel Hombroich near Neuss, Germany: wetlands restored.

One concern that landscape architects can help address is the fear we may be entering a sixth phase of species mass extinction, the so-called Holocene extinction. The most recent previous mass extinction was the Cretaceous–Tertiary extinction some 65 million years ago when dinosaurs disappeared. The current loss of species is related to human settlement, consumption of resources and anthropogenic (human-made) climate change. If only from a selfish point of view, mankind should be concerned about biodiversity because if there is no room on the planet for other species, there may soon be no room on the planet for *Homo sapiens* either.

Inspired by such ecological thinking, the latter part of the twentieth century has added a wider responsibility – that of sustainability – to the idea of respect for a particular place. Sustainability is most commonly defined in the terms of the 1987 Brundtland Commission as 'meeting the needs of the present without compromising the ability of future generations to meet their own needs'. This embraces two conflicting concepts, that of needs (implicitly those of the world's poor), and that of placing limits on the environment's development and hence its capacity to meet present and future needs. This relates to the idea of mankind's ecological footprint and the capacity of our planet to support present human activity and, indeed, life generally. It is forecast that we are consuming resources unsustainably: for instance, at present rates of consumption the supply of oil will be exhausted in the next 30–40 years according to many industry authorities.

Underlying our exploitative use of the Earth's resources is the world's growing population (over seven billion at the time of writing in April 2012), projected by the UN to grow to up to 10.5 billion by 2050. In 1947, when the older of this book's two authors was born, the world's population stood at 2.5 billion.

Landscape architects can play a particular tactical role by giving *meaning* to the fine words on sustainability found in many public and private corporate statements; they can help translate political rhetoric into practice. To give one obvious, highly practical, everyday example: rigid, inflexible paving laid on a concrete foundation uses far more embodied carbon and energy than flexible paving laid on stone aggregate foundations.

Industrialization and international trade have led to the growth of urban settlements and to changes in the way the countryside is used. Landscape architecture responded initially by focusing on the provision of recreational space, both public and private, and on general 'city beautification', and then by broadening its remit to encompass managing the impact of a changing society on the wider landscape. This in turn led to the protection of natural areas, such as in national parks. Olmsted was one of the commissioners for the proposed Yosemite reservation in 1864–66. Most recently, this has led to a concern for the whole landscape, including industrial and non-designed or vernacular landscapes.

The new purpose-built public municipal parks (a nineteenth-century innovation) provided the initial impetus for the development of both the discipline and profession of landscape architecture; environmental legislation has since widened its role. For instance, the 1946 British New Towns Act led to a whole generation of British landscape architects working on new town masterplans. Post-war German *Bundesgartenschauen* or Garden Festivals were used to regenerate German cities. The 1984 Liverpool International Garden Festival was a British import of this policy made in reaction to civil unrest. The International Garden Festival was a world exposition and it attracted nearly four million visitors.

International or transnational legislation such as the European Community Directive on Environmental Assessment (1985) has also benefited landscape architecture practice – so much so that some landscape architects now specialize in Environmental Assessment (see below). The landscape received its most emphatic international political imprimatur in 2000 in the form of the Council of Europe's European Landscape Convention (see Appendix 2: 'The significance of legislation and conventions, national and international and the European Landscape Convention'). This commits countries to preparing inventories of the entirety of their landscapes, not just special areas of natural interest such as national parks, and to promoting landscape (and thus, implicitly, landscape architecture) education.

As the growth of the profession reflects, landscape architecture is well placed as a discipline to address the problems caused by industrialization and rapid urbanization and the consequent changes in the countryside in India and China. Since the 1960s landscape architecture has increasingly been concerned with ideas of sustainability, ecological health (including derelict and toxic land) and global warming, biodiversity, population growth and the ecological footprint.

When designing external spaces, architects and developers tend to focus on buildings, which are relatively finite and made of dead materials; by contrast, landscape architects focus on the spaces between buildings. Landscape architects have a primary concern with site and a wish to embrace living processes, ecological systems and change, and base their ideas on an understanding of the natural world. Due to this holistic base, landscape architecture is a profession with the potential to help address the problems caused by humankind's impact on the planet.

The principles of landscape planning are now incorporated in various types of legislation and policy documents. In the US, the National Environmental Policy Act of 1970 was influenced by the work of Ian McHarg on Environmental Impact Assessment (EIA). EIA began in the 1960s in the US and was then applied to the development of the North Sea oil fields from the early 1970s onwards. EIA is defined by the International Association for Impact Assessment (IAIA) as 'the process of identifying, predicting, evaluating and mitigating the biophysical, social, and other relevant effects of development proposals prior to major decisions being taken and commitments made'. In 1985 assessments of this kind were made mandatory across what is now the European Union, where it is referred to as Environmental Assessment. In 2002, Strategic Environmental Assessment (SEA) was introduced in the European Union, subjecting economic plans and policies to a similar type of prior investigation.

Environmental Assessment is by its very nature multidisciplinary, and landscape architects have a specific role in it given that they are the only profession educated to assess the visual aspects of the landscape. Indeed, visual impact assessment has a wider application in relation to assessing the impact of any development. Landscape architects establish a baseline assessment of the existing landscape character, undertake a ZTV (Zone of Theoretical Visibility) mapping and then assess the visual impacts and how these can be managed, reduced or enhanced, all accompanied by photomontages or three-dimensional visualizations.

In China, the Environmental Impact Assessment Law of 2002 is starting to have some impact. In Asia, major development projects are taking place and illustrate the need for good landscape planning. The Three Gorges Dam on the Yangtze River, for example, has had an extensive impact on the landscape. This has been planned for to a degree, but future monitoring of the project is likely to show that better landscape planning and design might have been possible.

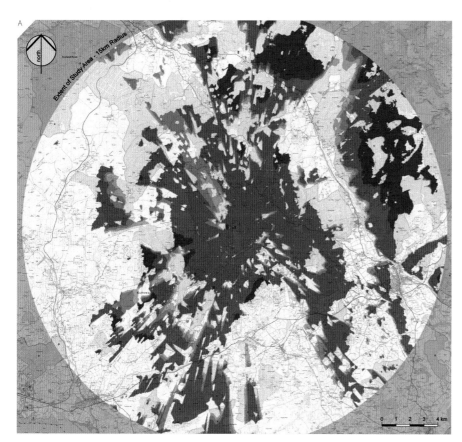

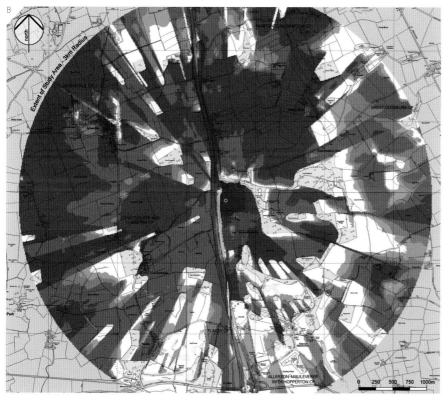

A. Example of a 15km-radius, multi-point, composite radial line ZTV analysis for a 60m single wind turbine located at the centre of the circle, shown on an Ordnance Survey 1:25,000 map base. The turbine is most visible from the areas that have the deepest blue colour.

B. Example of a 3km-radius, five-point ZVT analysis for a group of 44m-high industrial buildings with an 80m-high chimney located at the centre of the circle, taking into account existing visual (woodland) barriers. The buildings and chimney are most visible from the areas that have the deepest red colour.

Ijsselmeerpolders, the Netherlands

Making new land and landscapes

The Netherlands' history over the past 1,000 years has been one of claiming farmland from the sea. Set as it is in the Rhine delta the land reclaimed in the Dutch polders is highly productive. (A polder is a tract of land reclaimed from a body of water and usually enclosed by dykes.) First using windpower then from the nineteenth century using steam power, water was pumped out from larger and larger polders, leading to the reclamation of the Haarlemmermeer in the nineteenth century. The greatest opportunity was the Zuider Zee, an inlet of the North Sea. In the twentieth century the aim was for self-sufficiency in food production; the wartime famine of 1944–45 intensified this desire.

The *Rijksdienst voor de Ijsselmeerpolders* (RIJP) or Dutch State Office for the Ijsselmeerpolders was set up in 1918 and continued in operation until 1989. The works undertaken involved the enclosure or damming of the Zuider Zee by construction of the Afluitsdijk (literally 'enclosure dam'; 1927–32) and then the planned empounding of five main polders: first the Wieringermeerpolder, laid out as farms of 20ha; then the Noordoostpolder, laid out similarly to the Wieringermeerpolder, but including two islands, Urk and Schokland, which were to maintain their identity; third was Oostelijk Flevoland, laid out with larger farms and the new town of Lelystad as an administrative centre for all the new polders; and the Zuidelijk Flevoland, which included the new town of Almere, built as an overspill for Amsterdam. A further fifth polder, the Markerwaard, was planned and its enclosing dyke was largely built before the project was abandoned in 2003.

The first two polders, the Wieringermeerpolder and the Noordoostpolder, were contiguous with the mainland but groundwater problems were discovered, particularly in the much larger Noordoostpolder.

So the last two polders, the Oostelijk Flevoland and the Zuidelijk Flevoland, were reclaimed with clearwater lakes, the Veluwemeer and the Gooimeer respectively, varying from 500m to 3km wide between the new polder and the mainland. These lakes separate the new polders from the mainland and help maintain fresh groundwater levels in the old land.

The polders were all originally intended to be used for agricultural production. The reclamation process consisted of planting *Juncus* reed to dry out the drained land and establish a soil structure, then after two or three years the RIJP built drainage ditches and planted first rape, to suppress the reeds, and then cereal crops, to develop the soil and the fertility of the land. The land was then subdivided into farms and road and other services infrastructure was built. The Dutch State Forestry Service (the *Staatsbosbeheer*) took over both forestry land and the conservation areas. The forests of white willow (*Salix alba*), planted by the State Forestry Service, were as much for recreational use as for commercial exploitation. Increasingly, from the 1960s, land was devoted to nature conservation in the form of wetland areas.

The earliest polders were laid out traditionally, with tree planting providing shelter (particularly for cyclists) along all the roads. The villages reflected the Dutch vernacular tradition as reinterpreted in the twentieth century, so the houses had pitched roofs. This changed in the Oostelijk Flevoland, where the settlements had flat-roof Modernist buildings and the landscape was made much more open. The farm plot size was increased to 50ha with mechanization.

To the north-east of the Zuidelijk Flevoland, the Oostvaardersplassen is a 5,600ha nature conservation area of swamps, pools and shallow islands. This area was originally intended for industrial use and developed ruderal vegetation and fauna. It has drier and wetter areas and the dry part was initially a willow tree nursery. To graze this area, Konik ponies, red deer and Heck cattle were introduced, with the result that there is now a herd of 600 Heck.

The new polders in total increased the land area of the Netherlands by 5 per cent. So much so that by 1965 the Netherlands was self-sufficient in basic foodstuffs despite being one of the most densely populated countries in the world.

A

D

ministerie van verkeer en waterstaat   **rijksdienst voor de ijsselmeerpolders**

flevobericht
nr. 254   I

jaarverslag 1984 van de onderzoeksafdelingen van de
rijksdienst voor de ijsselmeerpolders

eindredactie dr. j. de jong

2130

E

B

C

Ijsselmeerpolders, satellite imagery of Zuidelijk Flevoland
with the mainland to the south, separated by the waters of
the Veluwemeer and the Gooimeer. The false colour imagery
has red for vegetation, with the brighter red indicating more
vigorous vegetation such as trees and reeds. Water is navy
blue. Built-up areas are pale blue and the bare soil of arable
fields is grey-green. The three views show the changing
development of the new polders.

A. 8 September 1980 satellite view: large arable fields
    seen as grey-green.
B. 23 May 1989 satellite view: fields have been subdivided,
    building work continues in Almere to the west.
C. 1 July 2006 satellite view: mid-year view, there are
    far fewer ploughed fields, Almere to the west has
    grown to a town of over 190,000 and the bright red
    Oostvaardersplassen conservation area with its lake
    is seen at the top.
D. Typical new polder view.
E. 1984 plan with the small Wieringermeerpolder (193km²)
    top left, the Nordoostpolder (469 km²) top right
    contiguous with the mainland, at the bottom Oostelijk
    Flevoland (528km²), and to the west Zuidelijk Flevoland
    (430km²).

2
Beginning a Project

Construction workers installing a major
water feature, Hong Kong.

This chapter sets out the initial stages of any landscape architecture project, beginning with the brief and proceeding through the positives and negatives of working with particular types of client, the various ways of estimating costs and the kinds of information that need to be gathered in a site survey. All of this work precedes the actual business of making a design, which will be covered in the next chapter.

The brief

A project begins formally with the brief, a description of the services the consultant is to provide for the client. This might be a one-page sheet or it might be a much longer document. Often clients may not know quite what they want or what a landscape architect can do; in such cases, the brief is often the result of a series of discussions between landscape architect and client. On the other hand, the client may have a great deal of commissioning experience and come up with a brief with little prior consultation.

The extent of the landscape architect's role will depend on their capabilities and on the project. Usually, however, the landscape architect will undertake the design and specification of the following for a building or engineering development:

- earthworks and mounds (with engineering advice for structural mounds such as road embankments);
- planting (i.e. trees, shrubs, herbaceous materials, grasses);
- topsoil or other soil;
- site grading and contours, including general levelling of roads and footpaths, working with engineers, and liaising with the architect on the ground-floor levels and siting of buildings;
- water features, e.g. lakes, swales, ponds and fountains;
- roads, footpaths and other paved areas in terms of their layout and appearance, including detailing kerbs, steps and path edges, again working with other consultants (in this case, civil engineers);

- design and specification of site furniture and fixings such as light fittings, seats and litter bins;
- liaison with the services engineers regarding location of services and trees, and
- monitoring the implementation by contractors.

Details will inevitably vary from project to project and from country to country. In the US, landscape architects often undertake earthworks engineering and plot layout for housing projects. However, landscape architects need to be careful not to accept responsibility for structural elements that are beyond their areas of professional competence, not least because of the insurance implications.

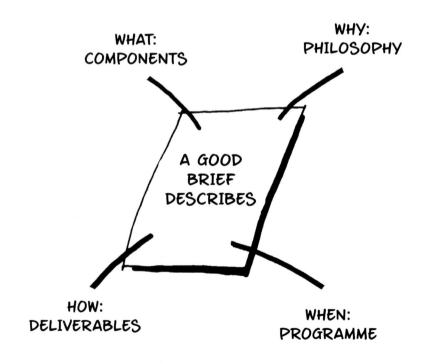

WHAT: COMPONENTS

WHY: PHILOSOPHY

A GOOD BRIEF DESCRIBES

HOW: DELIVERABLES

WHEN: PROGRAMME

A

C

B

Landscape architects need to develop an understanding of all the elements of a design.

A. Earthmounding, Venlo Floriade 2012, the Netherlands.
B. The potential of external lighting: simple fluorescent tubes mounted under the seats at La Villette, the design dates from the 1980s, nowadays LED lights are used.
C. Selecting plant material, Hilliers Tree Nursery, Hampshire, UK.
D. The seasonal colour changes of planting.

D

Therefore, while a landscape architect may design road layouts and propose the paving and draw the edgings and set the levels, he or she should ensure that a civil engineer is responsible for the structural aspects of the road, including the base make-up, and that services engineers design the electrical layout for the lighting and drainage of roads on any but the smallest projects. Public roads or larger road projects will require a highways engineer to undertake the layout design. Artificial lakes may well require the services of an engineer specializing in dam design.

At the earliest stage the landscape architect should visit the site and discuss the outline capital cost of a project. Indeed, costs should be discussed prior to agreement of the professional fees unless it is agreed to pay time-based fees for initial discussions. Professional fees are the payment for the professional services (pp.68–69) while contract costs are the monies paid to contractors to construct or plant the work (pp.141–44).

As an example, the landscape architects for the Paris EuroDisneyland theme park in 1990 were responsible for:

• sourcing of plants;
• design and specification of planting;
• design and specification of topsoil with some responsibility for advising on formation of engineered mounds;
• design and specification of irrigation;
• coordination of underground services (i.e. drawing them on plan and liaising with services engineers in order to ensure there was space to plant shrubs and trees);
• specification of backstage landscape maintenance areas;
• monitoring the work on site and reporting to the client.

The brief was predetermined by the client Walt Disney Imaginering (WDI) and their project manager, Lehrer McGovern Bovis, in a document of over 100 pages. The client wanted European landscape architects to ensure implementation of their design. WDI had designed three Disneyland theme parks beforehand. They knew what they wanted, but they did not know how it could be implemented in Europe. The whole design team visited the Los Angeles Disneyland and individual members were also delegated to visit the Florida and Tokyo versions. Morgan Evans, Walt Disney's original landscape architect, acted as a 'coach' on the tours and subsequently in Paris.

A. Landscape lighting in a scheme designed by Yann Kersalé, Musée du Quai Branly, Paris with methacrylate 3W LED light sticks varying in height from 30cm to 2m.
B. Earthworks, EuroDisneyland, Paris: the planted perimeter mounds are about 9m high and built to exclude the outside world.
C. Bank of China water feature, Hong Kong.
D. Planters, seats and interactive water feature at Venlo Floriade 2012, the Netherlands.
E. Wooden decking at Venlo Floriade 2012, the Netherlands
F. Stainless-steel reflection pool designed by Peter Walker, Town Center Park in Costa Mesa, California.
G. Timber boardwalk, Venlo Floriade 2012, the Netherlands.
H. Cutting granite paving, London.
I. Curved timber bench, Faro, Portugal.
J. Corten steel steps designed by Michael van Gessel, Grebbeberg, the Netherlands.
K. Hardwood terracing, Amsterdam.

C

D

E

F

G

H

I

J

K

Designers need to develop a confidence in planting and materiality.

A. Meadow planting, Venlo Floriade 2012, the Netherlands.
B. Mature tree planting, Liverpool One, UK.
C. Birch grove planting, London.
D. Mixed prairie planting, the Netherlands.
E. Autumn colour planting, Parc des Cormailles, Paris.
F. Bamboo planting, Le Jardin des Géants, Lille, France.
G. Large-scale perimeter earthworks, at EuroDisneyland Paris.

Landscape architects will need to work with a range of clients, both public and private.

A. Pre-cast concrete and timber benches, The High Line, New York: a public park, owned by City of New York, but run and operated by Friends of the High Line, founded in 1999 by local residents.

B. Screen wall lighting installation, Abu Dhabi: private developer.

C. Scalloped mounding and autumn leaves, Jardin Joan Miró, Paris: owned and managed with direct labour by the City of Paris (Ville de Paris).

D. Concrete swimming pool construction, Cyprus; private developer.

E. Lake earthworks under construction, Reading, UK: for a private-sector business park development.

F. Turfed amphitheatre terracing, Hedeland Arena, near Roskilde, Denmark: a public company, I/S Hedeland, an *Interessentskab* or partnership owned by the three surrounding local authorities, manages the area as a country park.

Types of client

The context within which landscape architecture is carried out varies according to the ways in which economies and administrative policies change. Hence, landscape gardeners in the eighteenth century worked for individual patrons; nowadays public and corporate clients are the norm. Clients vary and may be categorized as follows:

PRIVATE INDIVIDUALS (say, for a garden or estate or private house) can make the most challenging clients, especially if they are not used to construction and delays caused due to weather or late supply of materials. However, private clients can also be the most understanding, not necessarily wanting an instant result, and instead being prepared to wait for longer-term outcomes. The work can also be the most satisfying because you are providing a personal service, and you can transform their personal outdoor environment.

PRIVATE SECTOR DEVELOPERS: these may be industrial or leisure companies developing sites for their own occupation or may be real-estate developers of housing or offices or retail space, whether on a short-term speculative or longer-term basis. Real-estate developers may well have predetermined briefs and established ways of working that one has to comply with and that might prove problematic. Some of the best private developers are the landed estates, such as colleges or pension funds with a long-term interest in the land. For example, it was the private developer at Canary Wharf in London's Docklands who wanted a strong masterplan and a high-quality environment.

CENTRAL AND LOCAL GOVERNMENT, which will usually be like private developers in having predetermined ways of working. Often they make for challenging clients because their working methods can unduly limit design flexibility. One typical example would be a local authority requiring work to be completed to a tight timescale and at an inappropriate period of the year (whether too cold or too hot) because of financial-year or electoral considerations. Government projects can also be wide-ranging. The New Towns in the UK were government-agency developments and the *Rijskdienst voor het Isselmeerpolders* was the government body tasked with polder reclamation from the Zuider Zee in the Netherlands over seven decades. Some of the largest central-government bodies with large land holdings in the UK are the Forestry Commission and the Ministry of Defence, while in the US the National Parks Service manages 340,000km^2 of federal land.

NON-GOVERNMENTAL ORGANIZATIONS (NGOs) are not-for-profit bodies. In many countries, the largest of these are nature-conservation charities and foundations. They have a long-term interest in the stewardship of the land and therefore can make very good clients. Community and public-interest groups include bodies such as the Central Park Conservancy in New York, which is devoted to the upgrading of Central Park. In the UK the Painshill Park Trust is a local charity devoted to resurrecting an eighteenth-century landscape garden (see p.30). In Lisbon the Calouste Gulbenkian Trust is housed in a superb, 7-hectare Modernist park designed by Gonçalo Ribeiro Telles and António Viana Barreiro which it commissioned in 1968 with a lake, sculpture park and open-air theatre.

THE COMMONS

One issue for landscape architecture is that so much of its work involves what economists term common goods or 'commons'. Traditionally common land or alpine pastures and tropical forests (communally owned and shared) were seen as common goods. However, the definition is being extended to areas such as oceans, or Antarctica, clean air and water, or silence. Arguably the clean-up of the River Rhine in the past few decades linked with its decanalization can be seen as commons management and there are now concepts of global commons such as climate change and air quality. How to price or value these is a challenge for economists and for designers involved in their provision as well as society as a whole.

THE VALUE OF THE LONG VIEW

Often the best private-sector clients are those with long-term financial interests. Both banks and pension funds have money, and their challenge is to ensure the value of that money is maintained over the long term by good financial investment. One of our best clients was the former nationalized electricity pension fund Electricity Supply Nominees, for whom the challenge was to ensure the value of their investments would grow over a 40- or 50-year timescale: pensions funds are highly capitalized. This is a forester's timescale. Much more short-term in outlook are speculative developers who are interested in a quick return, selling on developments swiftly in order to generate more money to put into the next development. Universities, by contrast, can make wise and intelligent clients, but can also be difficult because they are staffed by highly educated specialists who may not have a good understanding of the property market or of design. The key to landscape architecture practice is building up a supportive client base. Remember too that clients often have ideals and you should live up to them.

Westergasfabriek Park, Amsterdam

Town council as client

Westergasfabriek Park in Amsterdam is a 13ha public park built for Stadsdeel Westerpark. The old Wester gasworks ceased production in 1967, leaving a highly contaminated brown-field site that by 1992 had fallen completely out of use. The area is only 3km from the centre of Amsterdam but is cut off on the north by railway lines. In the 1990s it was decided to develop the site for cultural purposes – rather than for housing or offices or other forms of commercial use – and that its role would be to serve all of Amsterdam rather than just the local borough.

Some of the industrial buildings had survived and could be converted for cultural or recreational use, and there was lengthy discussion about the standard of remediation required for the toxic materials in the ground. The brief was framed as a prestigious metropolitan development of a 'cultural/art/new media' type, with some 'community' facilities, set in a model ecopark. In January 2000 an agreement was made by Stadsdeel Westerpark (by then the landowners) to sell the site to a private developer for the equivalent of US$5 million, with the undertaking that they would renovate the industrial buildings and construct the park.

Gustafson Porter of London were selected as the landscape architects. The park was opened on 7 September 2003 by the mayor of Amsterdam, Job Cohen, and renovation of the old gasworks followed. The park had been turfed and planted with advanced nursery stock (i.e. quite big) trees in the hottest summer on record in Europe since at least 1540. The result was the death of over 90 per cent of the trees and turf. Clearly the designers had been overruled by the private developers so that the planting had taken place out of season. If the client had been better informed (in the way that the old City of Amsterdam Parks Department was), this would not have happened. This is a good example of a client insisting on inappropriate action for political or PR reasons. The park was subsequently replanted two years later. In 2007 it won the Landscape Institute's award for best park over 5ha in area.

A. Westergasfabriek: entrance bridge from the south across the *Haarlemmertrekvaart*, the seventeenth-century fast passenger boat canal to Haarlem with views of the old gasworks building beyond, now a cultural, music and film venue with Sunday markets outside.

B. Gustafson Porter's competition-winning plan arranged on an east–west axis, with a more naturalistic area to the north-west where it links with the earlier *Water Natuurtuin*, a peat wetland nature reserve. The east of the park is more formal with a large events lawn, and formal concrete-edged pool for summer wading and play. To the east are the existing Westerpark gardens, which date from 1891 when the area was first developed.

C. View of the stream and 'valley' to the west of the park.

D. Though the two pools may seem one, in fact the wading pool and the cypress pool are totally separate, the wading pool fed with clean water, while the latter takes surface drainage water and is part of the water-cleansing system.

E. View of the cypress pool with embankment and wading pool beyond. Swamp Cypress (*Taxodium distichum*) trees grow on individual mounds.

F. The cascade between the cypress pool boardwalk and the reed pool to the left; the cascade oxygenates the water.

G. The gasometer pool, planted with reeds and with islands for ground-nesting birds.

B

C

D

E

F

G

Fees: how to get paid

The capital values (the monetary value of the development contracts) for which a landscape architect is responsible are often small compared to those handled by other development consultants, such as engineers or architects. Therefore the cost and overheads of a landscape architect's attendance at a regular site or at design team meetings may be proportionally much more than the value of the work they are responsible for. The upside is that a landscape architecture practice is usually involved in more projects simultaneously than, say, an engineering or architectural practice, not only because of the smaller capital values of landscape projects, but also because the projects tend to last longer. When a building is complete and handed over to the client, the architect's involvement is usually at an end; by contrast, landscape architecture projects are often just beginning to develop when the clients take them over, so there can be continuing management consultancy roles for landscape architects. Financially this equates to smaller financial eggs put in a greater number of baskets.

It is also important to distinguish capital development costs from continuing management and maintenance costs. Management and maintenance is key to the long-term success of landscape projects as well. This can range from street cleaning and litter collection to painting and maintaining signs and railings, to horticultural maintenance from grass cutting to pruning trees and indeed the wide range of normal gardening. Lakes need dredging from time to time, fountains and pumps need regular maintenance as does lighting and painting of timber structures. All this has to be planned for and programmed from the beginning. And the revenue stream to pay for all this, and which may be service charges on rental property, has to be planned for.

Stuart Lipton, the developer of Stockley Park, in our view Britain's best-designed business park, once quipped that 'Landscape costs peanuts', yet he also realized that the attentions of a landscape architect can seriously enhance property values. That is, landscape architecture can make developers money. The challenge for the landscape architect is to ensure that their contribution is properly valued.

The overheads (e.g. travel, office costs, meals, and, if at a distance, hotel fees) in landscape architecture are always a challenge so it is wise to negotiate time fees for attendance at design meetings, site meetings, and plant nursery visits – which, remember, might well be abroad: major European centres for big tree production are in Pistoia, Italy, the Netherlands and Schleswig Holstein. If you are looking for large palm trees you may have to visit Florida or Spain. Elements that need to be established early on include:

a) an adequate estimate both of capital and ongoing maintenance costs;

b) a design programme – the timetable for the production of the designs and drawings, for costing purposes and then for a planning application and finally for production information so that contractors can tender for the work;

c) a tender programme – the timetable for competitive tendering. This requires selection of suitable companies, a reasonable period to permit tendering and then time to consider and check the tenders and appoint a successful contractor;

d) a site works programme – the programme of works with effective and realistic timescales, covering all work up to completion;

e) a maintenance programme with responsibilities and provision for continuing finance (through a planned revenue) of site maintenance and management.

Note that the cost estimate should come first. When first appointed, the landscape architect should ensure that the capital value is sufficient for the works. One of the authors of this book participated in the work for the first 56ha theme park at EuroDisneyland, now Disneyland Paris. The initial-stage landscape consultants, Clouston based in London with Paris-based API, were responsible for the planting, topsoiling, irrigation and services coordination. On being appointed, the landscape architects found that the prior allocation for the landscape works was 40 million French francs. A detailed cost estimate by the landscape architects based on outline drawings determined a cost estimate of 180 million francs: the final cost was in the order of 120 million francs. The initial cost estimate by the project managers was too low by a factor of three. Cost estimation should always be made on the basis of comparable projects and land area.

Sometimes a client does not know who will be responsible for the ongoing management of a project. For example, the London Docklands Development Corporation (LDDC) presumed that the local London borough of Newham would take on the management of the Thames Barrier Park (see p.74) when it was completed in 2000. However, management costs money and the LDDC had failed to put any financial arrangements in place for the site's ongoing management so Newham refused to take over the new development. The LDDC could have made such financial arrangements a covenant as part of its planning permission, or built a service-charge arrangement into subsequent land sales (it was the landowner as well). The adjacent private housing developments could have helped finance the maintenance of the park – not inappropriately since they benefit from the park. In consequence the opening of the park was delayed and ultimately the newly founded Greater London Authority, under the Mayor of London, took over responsibility.

FEES

There are three main ways of charging for consultancy work: time, percentage and lump sum.

TIME CHARGES can be at an agreed hourly, daily or weekly rate for each grade or individual member of staff, including principals, and will vary depending on staff experience and responsibilities. There should also be review dates, especially for long projects and in times of high inflation – fees can be index-linked. Index linking involves relating agreed fees to an agreed price index whether cost of living, national wage levels or construction industry costs so the rise is in line with inflation over the months and years. Time charges (which might be to a pre-agreed limit) are particularly appropriate for early-stage work or for desk studies such as environmental assessment or landscape planning work. They are a secure way of assessing fees.

PERCENTAGE FEES relate to the value of the work and are usually a percentage of the total cost of a contract or subcontract for which the landscape consultant is responsible. For instance, a £1,000,000 landscape project might require 5–10 per cent fees which would be £50,000–£100,000. Alternatively it might be a much lower percentage, say 0.5 to 10 per cent, of the total capital cost of the whole project, particularly if the landscape architect is advising on the location and orientation of buildings or the masterplan framework for road and other engineering work. Percentage fees generally also vary with the complexity of the type of work and the size of the capital sum. Lower-value projects rate a greater percentage of the total value in fees; greater complexity likewise justifies a larger percentage fee. For example, golf courses, country parks and forestry schemes are generally considered less complex, while urban design or historic landscape conservation are considered the most complex. Most landscape architecture professional bodies have guidelines for percentage fees.

LUMP-SUM FEES are fixed sums, they often include expenses (which should be costed as at least an additional 10 per cent of the total fee), and are preferred by many clients who wish to have a firm idea of costs. The initial calculation is first made on a time-fee or percentage basis and then converted to a lump sum. However, there has to be a clear agreement as to the timescale (and allowance for delay in the total project), prior agreement as to what happens if there is a change of brief (called a 'change order', which involves an extra fee for extra work) and allowance for inflation.

There is a fourth kind of financial arrangement, made on a retainer-fee basis. This is for when a client wants to retain the services of a landscape consultant on an 'as-needed' basis over an extended period of time, during which all work arising is required to be carried out by the landscape consultant. But, again, there has to be a clear definition of the extent of the work.

PAYMENT STAGES – Stage payments can apply to all methods of fee calculation and each stage fee is best invoiced monthly, based on the current timetable for design and implementation. This ensures an adequate inflow of money and means that you are not having to wait an undue time for payment, say, because of a delay in a project or because the client prefers to release payment slowly.

Stage fees break up the design and contract implementation programme of a development into various letters phases or stages, for instance as below. The Landscape Institute's current percentage stage fees are:

WORK STAGE		PROPORTION OF FEE	TOTAL FEE
A	Inception	N/A	N/A
B	Feasibility	N/A	N/A
C	Outline proposals	15%	15%
D	Sketch scheme proposals	15%	30%
E	Detailed proposals	15%	45%
F/G	Production information and bills of quantities	20%	65%
H/J	Tender action & contract preparation	5%	70%
K	Construction	25%	95%
L	Completion	5%	100%

Percentage fees are not appropriate for stages A and B, and these stages should be charged on a time-fee or lump-sum basis (it does not imply they should be done for free). You could say that each should be charged at 5 per cent .

Central Park, New York City

Charity as client

Central Park is a 341ha city park in the centre of New York City, initially opened in 1857, it was designed by Calvert Vaux and Frederick Law Olmsted. By the 1970s it had become run-down. In 1980 the Central Park Conservancy was founded, a private, not-for-profit organization, which included a group of civic and community leaders and aimed to restore, enhance and manage Central Park in partnership with the City of New York.

In a power-sharing arrangement between the city council and the charity, the Central Park administrator serve as the chief executive officer of the park and of the Conservancy. In 1979 park commissioner Gordon J. Davis appointed Elizabeth Barlow Rogers as the Central Park administrator. Rogers was a park activist and the author of books and articles on parks and Olmsted. Davis asked Rogers to raise money from the private sector to cover her own salary as administrator. In 1980 this arrangement was formalized with the creation of the Conservancy. From 1982, Rogers oversaw a team of landscape architects as they undertook a three-year survey of all aspects of the park. This led to the creation of a masterplan. The plan included the restoration of the park's Sheep Meadow, the planting of thousands of shrubs and flowers, and the restoration of significant structures such as the Bethesda Terrace and Fountain and the Belvedere Castle. It proposed spending $150 million on a 'systematic and coherent renovation' in a ten- to fifteen-year period. By the end of its first decade, the Central Park Conservancy had raised more than $65 million for this public-private venture, contributing more than half of the park's budget and exercising substantial influence on decisions about its future.

In 1998 the Conservancy and the City formalized their partnership. Currently the Conservancy is responsible for the day-to-day maintenance and operation of the park. It employs 90 per cent of the park's maintenance operations staff, and provides 85 per cent of its $42.4 million annual management budget through fundraising and investment. In addition to paying an annual fee to the Conservancy for the services it provides, the City funds lighting, maintenance of the park's drives and law enforcement. Central Park now has 35 million visitors a year and the Conservancy is a model for the renewal of a historic city park by a public-private partnership.

A

The 341ha New York Central Park.

A. Looking across the lake to the Central Park
    West Corporation building.
B. View from the Central Park Conservancy towards
    the south-west.
C. The Sheep Meadow in context with the backdrop
    of 8th Avenue and the Theater District.
D. Looking north towards Harlem, with the Sheep
    Meadow, the lake and the Jacqueline Kennedy
    Onassis Reservoir engulfed in the tree canopy.
E. The long view down the lake towards
    Central Park South.

Site survey

Knowledge of site is the basis of landscape architecture and it should be gained by both direct observation and research into records and published plans; in this way, an understanding can be built up that is both factual and emotional. It is essential to walk a site, experience it at different times of day and year, and record its elements. Ideally one should also sleep on the site, though this is not entirely usual practice – but on the one occasion we slept on a site, we won the international design competition.

The site survey should record the physical features on the site. Often the ground survey, which includes details of existing contours, built structures and the main vegetation, will be carried out by a specialist surveyor, but this should always be supplemented by a landscape survey to ensure that the landscape architects themselves gain a thorough knowledge of the site. A full landscape site survey will involve a ground survey by the engineers to show the bearing capacity of the soil and groundwater levels and may involve a detailed tree condition survey by an arboriculturist (a tree consultant).

A site survey should look at/include the following elements:

*   geology and surface geology;
*   site soils, infertile and fertile soil;
*   hydrology, water table and surface water, e.g. pools, streams and rivers, flooding, shorelines and tidal areas with high and low tides;
*   climate and microclimate, sunny aspects, frost pockets, areas exposed to wind, sheltered areas, sun-path diagram, the latitude and longitude of the site;
*   vegetation including grasses, herbaceous and woody vegetation, and significant habitats; individual trees and woodland;
*   site history: historic and listed (or protected) buildings, structures and artefacts;
*   site use, both formal and informal, and regular and occasional;
*   views in, out and within; and types of view such as extensive panoramas or views to landmarks;
*   site surfaces, buildings and artefacts; note building materials including stone, the bond of brickwork, type of mortar, colour and texture, paint colours;
*   site services: drainage, electricity, water, telecommunications, gas, etc;
*   climate: wind, rain, temperature, exposure;
*   topography and levels, contour survey of the site, steep slopes;
*   photographic survey;
*   noise and pollution, both ground and air pollution;
*   planning and ownership status, building covenants, planning controls and designations.

In addition, the site should be placed in its social, environmental, ecological, economic, transport and historical context so that the external factors affecting it can be evaluated. For example, the presence and capacity (or absence) of services such as mains electricity or sewers may facilitate or restrict the nature of a development. Proximity to employment, schools and shops and transport is an important factor in housing projects, while the presence of special habitats or sites of historical or archaeological significance may restrict the scope of, or offer extra opportunities to, a particular development.

Survey plans may then be collated and analysed in the form of a composite plan, usually referred to as an opportunities and constraints plan, or sometimes a SWOT analysis (Strengths, Weaknesses, Opportunities and Threats).

Only after all this information has been collected and organized can the actual design work begin. Landscape architecture is nothing without knowledge of site: it is vital to visit, to breathe in and understand a site, take time, sleep on it if you can, live on it is better and certainly experience it at different times of the day. Without an adequate understanding of the site, one may proceed with a design that ultimately proves unworkable or extremely expensive to implement.

SITE ELEMENTS
TO BE RECORDED

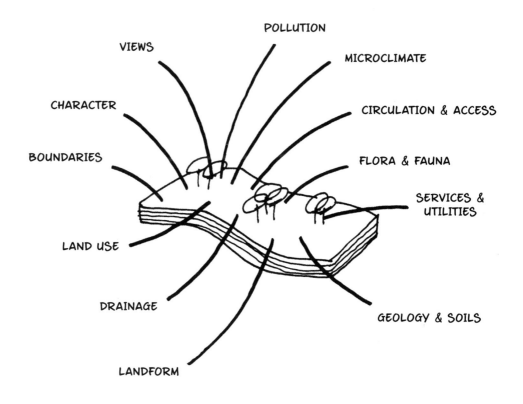

POLLUTION

VIEWS

MICROCLIMATE

CHARACTER

CIRCULATION & ACCESS

BOUNDARIES

FLORA & FAUNA

SERVICES &
UTILITIES

LAND USE

DRAINAGE

GEOLOGY & SOILS

LANDFORM

A. Site survey drawing

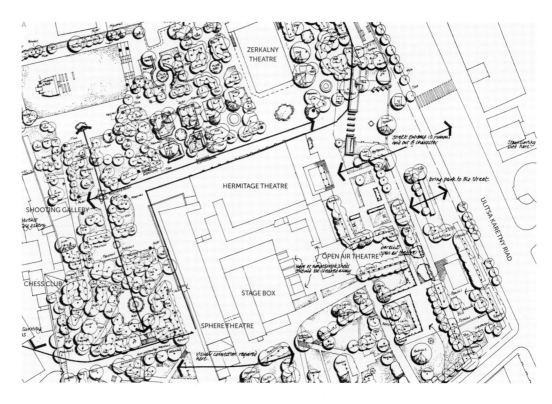

ZERKALNY
THEATRE

HERMITAGE THEATRE

SHOOTING GALLERY

OPEN AIR THEATRE

ULITSA KARETNY RIAD

CHESS CLUB

STAGE BOX

SPHERE THEATRE

Thames Barrier Park, London

Public-sector development corporation as client

This project represented the idea, new to post-war London, that public urban park investment could lead to the wholesale redevelopment of an area. The park is characterized by a green dock, reflecting the historical use of the site, copses of trees and concrete paths. The Thames Barrier Park was intended to encourage private housing in the adjacent plots. This has happened to the west and east, although the Pontoon Dock site to the north on the far side of North Woolwich Road remained empty and vacant at the time of writing.

The park's uses are traditional and mainly passive: it is a place for walking, for horticultural display and for enjoying views of London – the Thames Barrier, the river itself and tree-clad Shooters Hill to the south. The site fronts the north bank of the River Thames just west of the Thames Barrier. The post-industrial site of the park in Silvertown had a legacy of pollution, particularly oils and tars. The Greater London Council had proposed a park in 1984, an idea adopted by the London Docklands Development Corporation (LDDC), which acquired the site in 1995, and it launched an international two-stage competition for the reclamation of the derelict and toxic land and development of a park and residential scheme. At this stage there was no set budget.

The London-based architect Patel Taylor and the Paris-based landscape architect Groupe Signes won the competition, with Arup as engineer. The Groupe Signes team were led by the French landscape architect Allain Provost, who had designed the Parc Diderot at La Défense and the Parc Citroën-Cévennes in Paris.

Meanwhile, in 1998 the LDDC had been wound up and the park passed first to English Partnerships (another central-government agency) and then to the new mayor of London and the Greater London Authority (GLA) in July 2000. The park is now owned and maintained by the GLA and park maintenance is under contract.

The overall tender price was just over £8 million, which came from the LDDC, English Partnerships and the London Borough of Newham. As developed, the park is much as the original design envisaged. It covers 9.3ha and this gives an all-in figure of £86/m^2 compared with the £300/m^2 for the Parc de Bercy in Paris, an eastern Parisian equivalent, also sited next to a river.

The Patel Taylor/Groupe Signes design was for a simple, square-shaped grass plateau fronting the Thames, with housing development on three sides. The housing blocks were to be like 'armchairs': long, central façades bookended by two shorter blocks maximize views in and out. Most of this square plateau is mown grassland, but it is marked by patterns of long meadow grass and copses of birch trees. The original idea was for six white, red, blue and yellow wildflower meadow-grass areas, but this has not been realized and the long grass is dominated by green vetch. Wildflower meadow grass is challenging to achieve in public parks because people trample on it and it needs skilled management. At the Thames Barrier Park the imported topsoil proved to be overly fertile, causing the wildflower meadow to fail.

In the competition entry, the green dock had mounds rising and falling within it like waves to create a sense of mystery as one approached from the park entrance on North Woolwich Road. However, only one mound was actually built at the northern end. Now the view extends uninterrupted from the entrance across the whole park to the shapes of the Thames Barrier's bright, stainless-steel-clad piers. This green dock gesture is impressive at first, but on repeated visits can prove a bit anticlimactic since there is only one way in and one way out. Paths at the plateau level lead to connections to the high-level Pontoon Dock station on the Docklands Light Railway extension to City Airport opened in 2005. The elegant effect is typical of late Modernism. It is refreshing to see such a simple, confidently handled, truly contemporary park design in the UK.

A. The pavilion remembering the victims of WWII.
B. The remarkable green dock retaining walls clad in *Lonicera pileata*.
C. Between the hedges are monospecific block displays of flowering herbaceous plants.
D. View from the DLR railway station over the green dock to the river and the Thames Barrier (top left).
E. Green dock showing the wave pattern of the hedges.
F. Dying yew hedges in the green dock due to imported wet clay topsoil.

3
The Design Process

The Erin Business Park (built on the site of an old coal mine) in Castrop-Rauxel in the Ruhrgebiet, one of the Emscher Park IBA projects.

This chapter reviews design process and its basic elements such as the significance of site, of inspiration, hierarchy and human scale and human flow and natural change. It describes the five components that a landscape architect deals with, discusses ideas such as hierarchy, symmetry and asymmetry, national attitudes to landscape, human scale, linearity, colour, form and texture, and ideas of process and change.

Developing a design

The design process is the sequence of steps that a designer undertakes when responding to a commission. Sometimes this is logical, sometimes more intuitive and sometimes pragmatic. The sequence includes such things as design methods, skills and inspiration, which together form a focused programme of action.

General approaches to a brief might be simplified as falling into two categories: problem-based and solution-based. For example, a business park proposal might be framed in a problem-based manner: it has so much floorspace, with a predetermined road access network and a range of buildings with a similarly predetermined number of car park spaces related to floorspace (e.g. one car parking space/20m² of building floorspace). This helps define the consequent approach to the open space design, such as whether to provide wet balancing ponds (to cope with stormwater) or lakes and landscape areas or gardens for offices with a perimeter shelterbelt. By contrast, a solution-based approach might involve thinking of a business park as a place of work where creativity and teamwork might be enhanced by the design of the open space and the creation of an environment that provides relaxation from the meetings and computer-based activities of a normal office. This might offer a landscape garden setting and a regular opportunity to look away from the computer screen to take in a view of pleasing scenes with water and vegetation – a setting that encourages people to work together in groups with access to gardens for relaxation or meditation or for a place for discussion or trim trails or grouse or duck shooting or golf. The issues of access and site planning are then subordinated to this ambition. The argument here could also be that a better environment will give greater real-estate value.

Design ideas are often derived from the contextual nature of the site, the *genius loci*, understanding these different qualities help in the development of a design response and guide the design process.

A. The courtyard of the Mezquita de Córdoba, Spain.
B. The English picturesque: Painshill Park, Surrey, UK.
C. Post-industrial: Duisburg Nord Landschaftspark, Germany.
D. Desert shelter, southern Sinai Desert, Egypt.
E. Elevated viewpoint, Grebbeberg, the Netherlands, overlooking the Rhine flood plain.
F. Contemporary public realm, Liverpool, UK.
G. Karst limestone scenery, Guilin, China.

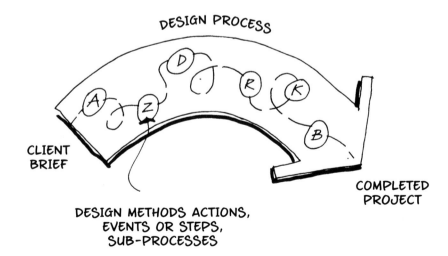

DESIGN PROCESS

CLIENT BRIEF

DESIGN METHODS ACTIONS, EVENTS OR STEPS, SUB-PROCESSES

COMPLETED PROJECT

A

B

C

D

E

Landscape architects need to be able to recognize function, scale, juxtaposition, and the enclosure of space as they evaluate context.

A. Multi-level retail public realm, Liverpool One, UK.
B. Patio de los Arrayanes, Alhambra, Spain.
C. Temple bathing pool, Bali.
D. Mémorial des Martyrs et de la Déportation, Notre Dame, Paris.
E. Renaissance courtyard grotto with cascade, Genoa, Italy.
F. King's College from the Backs, Cambridge, UK.
G. The Grand Axe crossing Paris viewed from La Défense.
H. Cataract, Nikko, Japan.

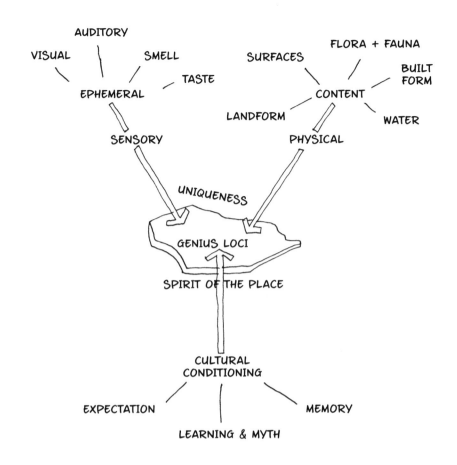

AUDITORY
VISUAL
SMELL
TASTE
EPHEMERAL

FLORA + FAUNA
SURFACES
BUILT FORM
CONTENT
LANDFORM
WATER
PHYSICAL

SENSORY

UNIQUENESS

GENIUS LOCI

SPIRIT OF THE PLACE

CULTURAL CONDITIONING

EXPECTATION
LEARNING & MYTH
MEMORY

Misty upland pasture, in the valley of Nant Cymdu, Aberdraw, Wales. The spirit of this place is that of Celtic culture, sheep farming and memories of the tailors who owned this field, and made flannel suits in their homes, using wool woven in local mills.

REVEALING THE SITE FOR THE DESIGN

There is an orderly sequence of techniques: for instance, site survey, analysis and design (known as SAD), the site as revealed by the analysis of the survey should in turn determine the design. For example, don't build on a flood plain, don't develop on steep slopes or areas of poor ground-bearing capacity or don't develop on existing areas of biodiversity value. In the 1960s Ian McHarg's sieve-mapping technique involved overlaying maps each showing different criteria to define the feasibility of different areas. Nowadays digital design including Geographic Information Systems (GIS) facilitate this technique. Sieve mapping involves mapping constraints and opportunities. Environmental Assessment is another rather similar design method. Such methods require understanding of a site, the development of form, following rules of composition, whether symmetrical or asymmetrical, and so on.

DESIGN SKILLS

These may be summarized as:

- thinking;
- problem solving;
- research;
- design;
- communication.

The necessary skills needed also involve the abilities to create a 'product' which could be in the form of:

- drawings;
- models;
- visualizations and walk-throughs;
- envisioning.

These can be analogue or digital or a combination of both. Drawings can be both freehand, mechanically drawn (i.e. analogue) or digital. Likewise, models can be real, three-dimensional objects or can be digitally created. Visualizations can be hand-drawn as in a comic book or film storyboard, or can be digital fly-throughs. Envisioning involves creating mental images of things or events by means of spoken or written cues or even by an event such as a community workshop. UDATs (urban design action teams) are precisely this sort of community action and from the beginning involve the community in generating ideas for a project.

DESIGN SKILLS

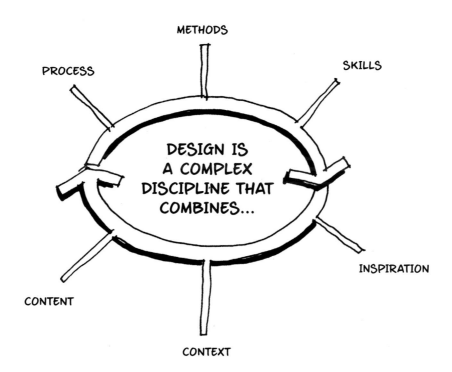

Derelict hill village,
Urbino, Italy.

DESIGN APPROACHES

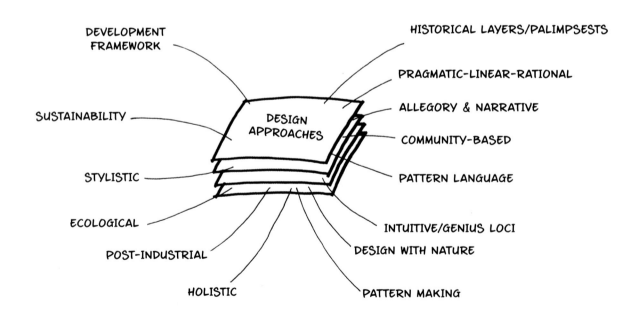

DEVELOPMENT FRAMEWORK

SUSTAINABILITY

STYLISTIC

ECOLOGICAL

POST-INDUSTRIAL

HOLISTIC

DESIGN APPROACHES

HISTORICAL LAYERS/PALIMPSESTS

PRAGMATIC-LINEAR-RATIONAL

ALLEGORY & NARRATIVE

COMMUNITY-BASED

PATTERN LANGUAGE

INTUITIVE/GENIUS LOCI

DESIGN WITH NATURE

PATTERN MAKING

INSPIRATION

This comes from all sorts of sources, and is usually a product of our wider lives, meaning the society in which one lives, the education one has had, cultural interests, etc. Clearly people living in dense urban areas, or countries with high population densities where land is much scarcer, tend to have different attitudes to people in more rural or less populated areas.

Nationally Americans and Russians who live in rural locations may have a very expansive view of the landscape because for them land is freely available; the American prairies or the Russian forest or tundra appear to go on for ever. The Dutch, the Danes or the Japanese have a much more managed approach in lands where space is limited. These are neat, man-made, tightly organized and managed landscapes.

American landscape architect Lawrence Halprin's work was influenced by his marriage to a choreographer so his design work has investigated ways of provoking an 'urban choreography' (including UDATs). The landscape design of the English landscape gardener William

Kent was influenced by seventeenth-century painting and the contemporary vogue for the Grand Tour of Italy which he undertook twice. Geoffrey Jellicoe was influenced by the early twentieth-century developments in psychiatry and the ideas of conscious and subconscious: some of his designs might be described as Jungian psychoanalysis-made-landscape. For instance Jellicoe described use of the subconscious in design thus:

'The process is simple. You first prepare a design in the normal way, you find it uninspiring, you place the drawing at a distance and preferably upside down, and you gradually become aware that it suggests a shape foreign but friendly to your own. In this shadowy shape you hope to discern some form that aspires to the perfection we call beauty (in the first three examples that follow are concealed animal forms, humans as symbolism, and allegory). You now reorganize the details of your design to conform (but not recognizably so) to the abstract idea within. Tell no one, if you can, for this is a message from one subconscious to another, and the intellect spoils such things.'

Later, in his Guelph lectures, Jellicoe defined five archetypes which he termed transparencies 'each carryng an imprint of the experience of an era':

1. *Rock and Water:* 'so remote as to be scarcely perceptible';
2. *Forester:* 'most small domestic gardens are inspired by the instincts of the *Forester*';
3. *Hunter:* 'from this idealistic transparency comes much of the English eighteenth-century Romantic landscape';
4. *Settler:* 'the era began through the discovery of geometry as a means of defining territory in an agricultural rather than a nomad economy... mathematics were divine';
5. *Voyager:* 'the unfinished transparency of our own era, which might be called the *Voyager* in contrast to the *Settler*'.

Such an approach is very different from the logical determinism of the SAD method, but that does not mean they cannot be combined.

INSPIRATION

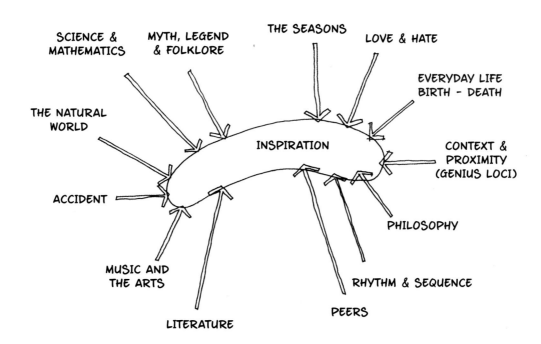

Aphrodite Hills, Cyprus

Tourist resort in a landscape of forestry and classical heritage

The Aphrodite Hills resort is a large 234ha integrated golf resort with five-star hotel, 18-hole championship golf course and villa housing (with individual pools) on the west coast of Cyprus near Paphos. Large beach resorts are not generally low-impact sustainable developments, so the challenge here was to minimize the adverse environmental effects, in particular on archaeological sites and forestry. Water supply was also an issue, since the island regularly suffers drought.

The site is in a particularly beautiful part of Cyprus, well treed and developed agriculturally. Crossing it is the Argaki Tou Randidiou ravine, with its maquis vegetation and Mammonia complex of rock formations. (Maquis is characteristic Mediterranean vegetation, with leathery, broad-leaved evergreen shrubs or small trees such as juniper, laurels, and myrtles.) No development is permitted here; the area is conserved as a landscape spine. The character of the Kapsalia and Dasia plateaux with both Lentisc (*Pistacia lentiscens*) and Kermes Oak (*Quercus coccifera*) dominating the maquis has thus been maintained.

The landscape is managed by the resort in conjunction with planning authority and forestry department requirements. There are footpaths allowing public access to the site and the surrounding forest. Construction in the ravine area is in the traditional Cypriot vernacular, with main features like the bridge being faced with local stone. In developing the resort road system, the intention was to reduce dependence on private car use and encourage walking, cycling and communal methods of transport.

Aphrodite has been designed as a sustainable resort community based on the local climate, ecology, topography and archaeological inheritance. Aphrodite is an important archaeological site so features have been protected. Cyprus has active forestry policies and the Mediterranean climate can be excessively hot in summer so shade was important. Active water features are self-contained recycling systems; pumps filter and recirculate the water. Energy-saving lighting was designed to minimize night-time ambient light pollution; visual comfort and the appreciation of the night sky were also priorities. This development is an illustration of landscape architects grappling with the potentially harmful environmental aspects of tourism in order to minimize its impact and maximize appreciation of the landscape's natural beauty.

A. Panoramic view from the east plateau showing the entrance road rising up the ravine to the village centre.
B. The 18th green and fairway flowing down to the golf club and village centre gardens.
C&D. The central ravine is protected from encroaching development.
E. The cascade in the hotel swimming pool.
F. Aerial view looking north of the golf resort visible in the green areas and the golf course on the hilltops, with hotel on the landward side of the Limassol–Paphos highway and linked to the beach by a passageway under the highway.

The principles of design

The five main components of a landscape plan are:

- vegetation: trees, shrubs and hedges, and herbaceous plants including grassland;
- vertical structures: buildings and other built forms including bridges and walls;
- horizontal structures: roads and paving;
- water: rivers, streams, ponds, lakes and shorelines;
- landforms: slopes, hills and valleys (described using contours and spot levels).

Site planning is the organization of a site to accommodate development using these components. The aim is to promote some form of human behaviour. It creates a pattern of the five main components in space and time, which then will change and grow and be subject to future management. Given this, the drawings, sketches, plans and specifications which the landscape architect produces are merely conventional ways of describing and communicating a forecast of this organizational complex in a physical form.

Landscape design is a type of futurology – a masterplan is a forecast of an ideal future image of a site, which will change in the process of implementation and thereafter. In truth, masterplanning is not so much a plan as a process. Any masterplan will change and develop. Therefore a favourite metaphor for landscape design is (again) that of the palimpsest, a manuscript that has been partially erased and then written over. This is obvious in many historic parks and gardens, where medieval fishponds have become formal lakes, before entering a more picturesque form and then perhaps silting up and drying out. Masterplanning is therefore best seen as a process whereby change to a site can be executed. Organizational structures (which may be roads or services lines) can be drawn diagrammatically and these may be adapted in response to context and function.

A. Vertical structures: shade pavilion,
    Zabeel Park, Dubai.
B. Horizontal structures: Exhibition Road
    repaved, London.
C. Horizontal structures: juxtaposition of timber
    and steel paving, Schouwburgplein, Rotterdam.
D. Water: cascading water feature and autumn
    leaves, UNESCO, Paris.
E. Vegetation: massed agapanthus planting and
    Corten steel façade, Córdoba, Spain.
F. Water: reflection pool, Mies van der Rohe
    pavilion, Barcelona.
G. Vegetation: clipped *allée* planting, Versailles, Paris.
H. Vegetation: planted roof terraces, Parc Güell,
    Barcelona.
I. Water: interactive fountain court, Somerset
    House, London.

A. Water: lakeside development, The Greens, Dubai.
B. Landform: sweeping grassed areas, Jubilee Park, London.
C. Landform: golf course landforming, The Centurion, St. Albans, UK.
D. Vegetation: mass herbaceous border planting designed by Piet Oudolf, Potters Fields, London.
E. Landform: Undulating play mounds at the Venlo Floriade 2012, the Netherlands.

HIERARCHY

Hierarchy in landscape design relates to the way elements are arranged to make some more dominant than others – say, the main streets of a town or the paths through a park. Hierarchical organization is a fundamental aspect of landscape design. Spaces may be sequenced and made dominant by means of their shape and size or by arranging their proximity to an entrance or transport node or by placing them on a symmetrical axis. The language used to describe designs may be broadly geometric (grid, axis, radial, orthogonal, centre) but common metaphors also relate to animal and plant structures (spine, head, arm, arterial, finger, node, branch, trunk) and clothing (belt, skirt).

Spaces may be defined by the use of mounds, by lines of trees, hedges and walls, and of course by buildings: most city spaces are enclosed by buildings – here landscape architecture overlaps with urban design. Bernard Tschumi in his prize-winning design for the Parc de La Villette in Paris defined the spaces using lines, surfaces and follies. The lines are paths, both straight and curvilinear, the *formes* (to use Tschumi's French) are surfaces, triangular and circular, enclosed by lines of trees, and his 'follies' are constructions on a 50m grid to provide a regular grid of points to structure the park. In Modern Movement gardens and landscapes such as Philip Hicks' Water Gardens in London of the 1960s (below), garden-scale

spaces are arranged geometrically, with the spaces demarcated by hedges, walls and rows of trees. While the spaces are simple in plan form, a variety of 'readings' – or ways of experiencing them – are possible. The overall order at Dan Kiley's La Défense in Paris is symmetrical, based on the straight *Grand Axe* that extends from there to the Tuileries in the centre of the city. The green spaces lie within the larger space formed by the office blocks on either side and provide a human scale. By contrast, in the Water Gardens, Philip Hicks organized the spaces around pools non-axially and are to be viewed as a whole from the apartments above. Hicks' asymmetrical organization is characteristic of the Modern Movement.

A. Hierarchy of elements: Tschumi's bird's-eye view plan of Parc de la Villette plan, Paris.
B. Vegetation: Dan Kiley's simple, square-grid plane tree planting at La Défense, Paris.
C. Hierarchy of elements: a Modernist design by Philip Hicks, built 1961–66 as roof gardens over basement car parks, space arranged orthogonally (at 90 degrees in plan) and asymmetrically, Water Garden, London.
D. Hierarchy of elements: The *Grand Axe*, Paris, a strong visual axis across the city.

Gardens or parks organised symmetrically around a central axis are characteristic of Italian Renassance garden design, but more recently of the Arts and Crafts movement. Such spaces can be considered almost as outdoor rooms, particularly the early twentieth-century private gardens at Great Dixter in East Sussex or Sissinghurst in Kent. Their public equivalent are the municipal parks of Thomas Mawson.

At a much larger scale, the post-war Dutch polders are organized on a formal spatial basis. There, the main discussion point related to the size of the consequent spaces. The smaller, older Dutch polders offered only restricted views, further restricted by roadside tree planting (to provide wind shelter for travellers); the much larger, later twentieth-century polder landscape by contrast opened up views to create a more expansive sense of the landscape, closer in feel to Canadian prairies, with high points such as church towers and power station chimneys viewed as orientation-giving landmarks. Redevelopment in the 1950s-70s was often highway engineer-led and resulted in the loss of pleasant, pedestrian friendly urban spaces. The growth of motor-car traffic in towns has tended to fragment the continuity of the enclosing buildings, roads have been widened and flyovers have cut across streets. In consequence, many urban spaces have now lost definition: town centres have become dominated by car parks and inner ring roads. Furthermore, building-plot sizes have tended to become bigger, so limiting flexibility of use and promoting uniformity of street frontage – which has consequently become less interesting. Perhaps the ultimate formal expression of this loss of urbanism or anti-urbanism is the town of Milton Keynes in southern England (see pp.148–49), which was planned around car-based travel, and where each grid square of housing or commercial development is hidden by surrounding tree-planted mounds (Milton Keynes is organized within a 1km-wide loose grid of roads).

Business parks such as Aztec West, near Bristol, attempted to deny their urban character by use of similar planted mounds alongside the main roads in order to give an impression of somewhere green.

Practitioners of the New Urbanism of the 1980s analysed urban form in terms of figure-ground plans, which show the built form as black and thereby emphasize the white spaces in between. The New Urbanism attempts to reverse this loss of urban character by increasing the density of settlements and re-creating enclosure and pedestrian-friendly spaces. Such re-establishment of the city as a pleasant place to walk and work goes back to the work of urban designers such as Jan Gehl in Copenhagen who worked on the pedestrianization of the main shopping street, the Strøget, in the 1960s.

A

SIMPLE ORGANIZATIONAL STRUCTURES

CENTRAL SPINE

GRID

PAN HANDLE/ LOOP

MAGIC WAND RADIAL

CONCENTRIC RINGS

FIGURE OF EIGHT/ DOUBLE LOOP

B

C

A. Six typical organizational masterplanning
    structures.
B&C. Clipped evergreen hedges defining garden
    rooms, Sissinghurst, Kent.
D. Water dominates the public spaces at
    Arlington Business Park, Theale, UK.
E. The main distributor road in Milton Keynes,
    the 'city of trees' has become a sort of blind
    anti-urbanism. This is in the middle of
    a town with a population of over 200,000.
F. At Arlington Business Park, Theale, UK,
    the entrance lake provides a strong business
    setting.
G. Early development view of Aztec West,
    a business park near Bristol, UK, showing
    the loop road configuration.

THE HUMAN SCALE

Landscape is land as perceived by humans, and its scale can be human or much bigger, overwhelming the human observer to create a feeling of grandeur or the sublime.

The term 'human scale' relates to human perception and may thus also relate to time, where a lifespan is about 70 years and a generation may be as short as 15. It may likewise refer to attention span, which can be minutes to hours, to temperature, to sound tolerance (anything more than 50 decibels is very noticeable, 130 decibels – aircraft take-off noise level – is approaching the pain threshold, but the quiet of the countryside can paradoxically prove unsettling for town-dwellers).

Landscape design at a human scale relates to the height and interval between steps, slopes, enclosures, path widths, walking distances and accessibility for the average human being – though, of course, median averages themselves may vary with age (children's gardens can be downsized) and nutrition.

The design of the buildings in Disneyland Main Streets uses theatre set design, and forced perspective to give an impression of height. The Main Street first storey is at three-quarter scale, then five-eighths scale at the second storey and half scale at the third storey. This gives a friendly almost toy-town like feeling while at first glance appearing full-sized. As Walt Disney said, 'No, it's not [just the way it used to be]… It's the way it should have been.'

Human scale can be overturned in landscape and urban design:

- for monumental and especially political effect: buildings, spaces and memorials can be constructed at an intimidatingly larger-than-life scale – which is what Hitler's Germany, Stalin's Russia and Ceaucescu's Romania did;

- for functional effect: many twentieth-century town planners and architects including some Modernists designed buildings and spaces to represent ideas of structural purity and clarity of form over 'concessions' to human scale: for example, landscape architects Sasaki, Dawson and DeMay's 1969 Copley Square in Boston, overshadowed by the Hancock Tower designed by I.M. Pei & Partners;

- in response to car use: buildings built to front highways tend to have simplified shapes and to be much smoother. The eye can take in about three objects per second. A passer-by steadily walking past a 30m frontage can perceive about 60 to 70 features; a car driver passing at 45kph can take note of just six or seven. Thus, in the face of increased car use, streets become bigger, urban form loses its complexity, signs grow larger and walkers feel more exposed (and literally are more exposed to winds and downdraughts). In the past 60 years cities have increasingly become less friendly to the pedestrian. It is as if we were deliberately setting out to design a dystopia.

The scale of space often defines its character.

A. The Scoop, City Hall, London: space as performance place, designed by Fosters.
B. Sunken seating spaces, The Serpentine Pavilion 2012, London.
C. La Grande Arche, La Défense, Paris.
D. The Burj Khalifa, Dubai: the 829.84m-high tower dominates the park.
E. Mémorial des Martyrs et de la Déportation, Paris.
F. The Serpentine Pavilion 2012, London.

STRAIGHT LINES AND CURVES

Linearity can be created in a landscape by juxtaposition of two surfaces, such as at the edge of a lawn, or by the use of a long, linear feature such as a canal or road. Landscape architects often design by drawing lines on a plan (as opposed to model-making or creating a sequence of storyboards) or with the assistance of vector-aided computer graphics (consisting of points joined by lines) which emphasizes this tendency to linearity. Reality is three-dimensional and two-dimensional plans undertaken without an appreciation of the third dimension can lead to flat design: designs that appear strong from above may be ineffective at ground level.

Straight lines are direct, strong and formal. Whether arranged symmetrically or asymmetrically, they guide the eye to an end point which may be given emphasis by a vertical termination. Diagonal lines are straight lines slanted across an orthogonal layout, as at the Parc Citroën-Cévennes in Paris. They may also be organized as a 60/30-degree plan layout as in many mid-century parks such as the 1970s Parc de Cergy-Pontoise, north-west of Paris. Nowadays the straight line is often seen as formal and manmade and therefore an 'unnatural' landscape element. Renaissance landscape gardeners such as Le Nôtre would not have agreed: they saw their formal, linear parks as an ideal representation of nature.

By contrast, curved lines tend to seen as informal, relaxed and natural. Use of the serpentine line began in the early eighteenth century in English landscape gardens, inspired by (what was thought to be) Chinese precedent. By the mid-eighteenth century the serpentine line had become standard in the Picturesque landscape garden. The eighteenth-century painter William Hogarth called it the 'line of beauty'.

By the mid-nineteenth century John Ruskin was asserting that 'all curves are more beautiful than right lines'. Curves were increasingly applied to both landscape and park design. City design was similarly influenced: for example, think of the curve of John Nash's Regent Street in London as it turns to meet Portland Place at the point marked by the vertical emphasis of the spire of All Souls Church, or the great descending curve of John Dobson's Grey Street in Newcastle upon Tyne. Such devices add a sense of mystery or discovery to a route, an effect that was well exploited by Humphry Repton in his park designs. In these, the curved approach path allows visitors to catch an initial glimpse of the house, usually across a lake, before swerving into woodland or behind mounds and tree clumps so that the residence is only seen again and more fully when they are much closer. The latter part of the nineteenth century saw a reaction against swerves and curves with the advocacy of the 'formal garden' by Reginald Blomfield, leading

to the imperial power of Edwin Lutyens' 1920s New Delhi and the triumphalism of Albert Speer's proposed *Ost–West Achse* (East–West Axis) in Berlin, which was planned to extend 50km in a perfectly straight line.

The mid-twentieth century saw a counterreaction to this and forms delineated by lines modelled on the human form (biomorphic lines) began to appear. Thomas Church's post-war California gardens such as Donnell Garden in Sonoma County characteristically used such curves, often complemented by similarly curved sculpture.

Verticality raises the eye to the sky – or to the heavens, where medieval cathedral spires are concerned. Such verticality can provide a town with a landmark – whether a cathedral or a skyscraper – or provide a park with an eye-catcher, as does Captain Grenville's Column in Stowe Gardens. Fastigiated trees can similarly provide an accent in a Picturesque layout or an emphasis in an avenue, like soldiers on parade.

Horizontal lines can give a feeling of expanse and rest or repose. They can unite a space and can be formed by low steps, walls, footpaths, terraces and wide lawns. Many Dutch landscape designs, such at that of the 1970s Oostelijk Flevoland, emphasize the horizontal in this way.

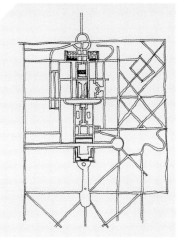

A. Sweeping lines of amphitheatre seating, Venlo Floriade 2012, the Netherlands.
B. Interlocking forms of marble sett paving, Porto, Portugal.
C. Controlled linear elegance of a temple entrance, Kyoto, Japan.
D. Formal mirror pool, Parc Citroën-Cévennes, Paris.
E. Overlaid grid and lines, Exhibition Road, London.
F. Sinuous granite edge, Jubilee Gardens, London.
G. The serpentine rill at Rousham, Oxfordshire, UK.
H. Informal gravel path reinforced by avenue planting, Venlo Floriade 2012, the Netherlands.
I. Vaux-le-Vicomte, Ile de France, designed by André Le Nôtre, with straight axes and a lattice pattern of paths in the woodland.
J. Parc Citroën-Cévennes, Paris: straight, orthogonal (right-angle) plan cut across with a diagonal.

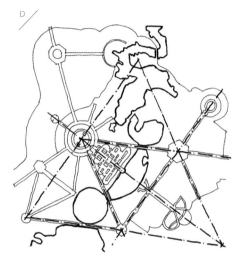

UNITY, HARMONY AND (A)SYMMETRY:

Consistency and simplicity are ways of achieving a harmonious effect in a landscape design. This might involve minimizing the number of materials used, avoiding clutter, massing plants and employing strong effects, such as water, tree lines and paving lines, very simply.

Symmetry involves positioning objects of equal value – whether size, height or form – on either side of a central point, axial line or surface. Symmetry denotes balance and order, and therefore, for some, is a divine principle.

Biological symmetry is common in multicellular organisms, usually as bilateral symmetry, in which body parts are repeated along a central vertical axis in one plane like a mirror image or as in butterfly-wing patterns. It can also be radial or rotational, as in flowers or arrangements of leaves on a branch. However, in nature such symmetry is rarely perfect.

Bilateral symmetry is common in landscape design, as in an avenue or axis, but balance can also be achieved through horizontal repetition, as in mirror pools as well as in vertical structures such as the Pont du Gard in southern France, where the storeys of arches repeat. Rotational symmetry as in a flower appears in Beaux-Arts-type circular plans such as W.B. Griffin's 1913 plan for Canberra.

But symmetry can also be applied to geometrical pattern making, as in Arab tile or paving patterns. One can construct landscapes using such geometrical repetition (as in C. Th. Sørensen's work (see above right)) and find symmetry in number theory and in the helix and double helix. The symmetry found in mechanics, quantum mechanics, the Standard Model of particle physics, relativity theory and cosmology can be applied to landscape design, as is the case with Charles Jencks's Garden of Cosmic Speculation, near Dumfries in Scotland.

At a much more basic level, patterns using the square, hexagon and equilateral triangle can be applied to landscape design in both detail and at a larger scale.

Asymmetry is the absence of symmetry, the lack of equality between parts. In the 1930s and 1940s James C. Rose, Garrett Eckbo, Thomas Church and Dan Kiley used orthogonal asymmetry as a way of aligning their work with Modernism, and as a reaction to the ruling symmetrical Beaux-Arts style. Later Kiley tended to absolute symmetry and a use of formal geometry. At a garden scale, the keynotes are planar walls, interplay between interior and exterior, emphasis on the horizontal (flat roofs and rectangular pools); and at the wider, landscape scale, interflowing spaces, and overlapping elements in plan.

A. Directional pebble mosaic, Mezquita de Córdoba, Spain.
B. Picturesque harmony of Compton Verney, Warwickshire, UK.
C. The Geometric Gardens, Herning, West Jutland, Denmark, 1983, designed by landscape architect C.Th. Sørensen.
D. The rotational symmetry of the Canberra masterplan of 1913 by Walter Burley Griffin of triangles with linking circles or *ronds-points* draped over the hills; it is now counterpoised by the water axis of Lake Burley Griffin, created in 1964.

COLOUR, FORM AND TEXTURE:

Landscape design deals with colour, texture and form, which may be described or defined by lines, mass and shapes to create space. As in architecture, but unlike film or proscenium arch theatre design, landscape architecture is experienced by the audience (the users) as they move through it. Unlike architecture, however, the components of landscape change because they include living biological forms. This dynamism is what can make landscape architecture with its living walls and moving roofs so much more exciting than a static architecture,

COLOUR has three main qualities: brightness, saturation or intensity, and hue. Hue is the quality of red, green, yellow or blue in a colour; saturation is the intensity of white or grey in a colour; the brightness of a colour is its luminance or reflectivity. So an intensely green landscape such as an English landscape garden in spring can appear bright, while a grey urban square can apprear drab, especially when empty. Brick buildings can be soft reds and oranges. The use of Luis Barragán-style planes of bright pink, reds, yellows as a stylistic feature of gardens and landscape designs became popular in the early twenty-first century.

FORM is the three-dimensionality and shape of an object. It may be regular, precise and human-made, or organic and natural in form (biomorphic). Natural forms may be controlled and fixed by clipping or by breeding, so, for instance, regular mop-headed trees can be grown by cloning.

TEXTURE has both tactile and visual qualities. Paving can be rough or smooth, and roughness may be desirable to prevent surfaces becoming slippery. Plantings similarly can be rough or smooth.

Clipped hedges demonstrate the differences between landscape and architecture. A formal clipped hedge, such as those of a French parterre, may be thought to be finite and unchanging. But even in this most controlled and architectural form of garden design there is constant change: hedges grow and become looser and more coarsely textured through a season and change colour and, of course, serve as a habitat for insects and birds and provide cover for mice. So, although they can be used to create 'rooms' in an unroofed house or palace, the result is far from an architectural construction.

Textures vary greatly depending on plant species, from the long thin leaves of *Oleander* to the sharp prickly danger of holly to the frilly foliage of *Chamaecyparis*. Living compositions can be placed alongside constructed walls, paving and pools, paving can be patterned and pools can be reflective, there are endless possibilities for composing these effects.

A. Japanese gardens often contain a simple harmony of elements, Kyoto, Japan.
B. Asymmetrical repetition of clipped yew topiary, Rodin Museum, Paris.
C. Complex harmony often contains many elements, in situ concrete path, Jardin Atlantique, Paris.
D. Transformation of form: clipped box hedges, Parc Diderot, Paris.
E. Combination of textures, Parc Diderot, Paris.
F. Contrast of material textures, Daisen-in Temple, Kyoto, Japan.
G. Association of colours and leaf textures, the Mehdi Garden, Hadlow College, Kent, UK.

ELEMENTAL DESIGN CRITERIA
OF AN OBJECT

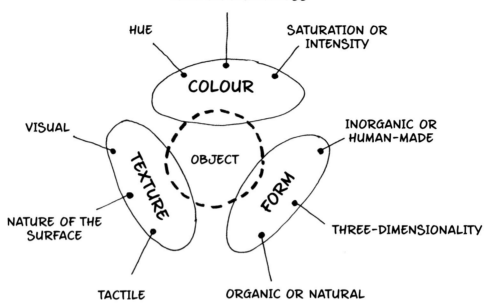

INFLUENCES ON DESIGN OF A HEDGE

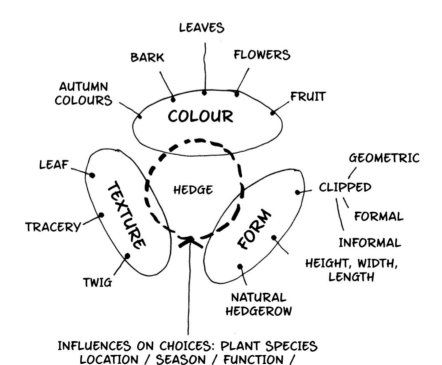

Understanding the elemental design selection criteria of the properties of materials develops a rationale for use. When applied to hedge materials these influences guide species choice.

A. Clipped beech tree blocks displaying autumn colouring, Parc André Citroën, Paris.
B. Autumn colour used to reinforce linear edge, Parc André Citroën, Paris.
C. Ordered complexity of marble sett paving, Faro, Portugal.
D. Japanese gardens use colour change as focal features.
E. Hot herbaceous planting exploring texture and form, Venlo Floriade 2012, the Netherlands.
F. In situ concrete with bamboo texturing.

Hedeland Arena, Roskilde, Denmark

A post-industrial landscape

East of Roskilde, on Denmark's main island of Zealand, is a 1,500ha gravel and clay extraction site. A brickworks opened here in 1897, with gravel-working operations following. The result was a crazy carving of the landscape-made-moonscape into a series of hummocks, hills and lakes which contrast with the broad, rolling, fertile fields that surround it.

Interressantskab Hedeland (I/S Hedeland), set up in 1978, is the body responsible for the redevelopment of this post-industrial landscape. It oversees land purchase, planning, construction and management. Gravel extraction continues on the site but is now interlaced with an extensive recreation development, which serves the area to the south and west of Copenhagen.

Thanks to I/S Hedeland's interventions, this sublime moonscape has been transformed in part into the short mown grass of an eighteen-hole golf course, and in part into woodland and nature areas. There is a network of bridlepaths, footpaths and cycle tracks along with a narrow-gauge tourist railway. I/S Hedeland has also planted a vineyard and developed wildflower meadows, a motor cross centre, arboretum, allotment/weekend leisure gardens and scout camp.

Because the topsoil has been lost, it is possible to create an extremely diverse and species-rich mix of woodland, scrub and grasslands on the subsoil and gravel material. The tree planting will eventually be dominated by oakwood (*Quercus*) and alder (*Alnus*). No herbicides and fertilizers have been used.

Rising out of the middle of the gravel-working site are a ski-slope mountain by Lea Nørgaard & Vibeke Holscher and a great arena of bright, green grass terraces which Is the brainchild of Erik Juhl, who is director of I/S Hedeland. The intensely green and formal landform contrasts with the loose piles of sorted gravel. The new outdoor arena has a red and white pre-cast concrete circular performance area backed by a strip of white gravel, which marks the area off from the gravel works behind. It accommodates 3,500 spectators and performances include pop, classical and ballet. One-metre-high, 45-degree grass sloped terraces rise 20m above the red and white circle in a great arc. A mound at the top of the terraces controls access and entry is via gatehouses built of turf and timber. Beyond and on axis are toilet blocks, also turf-walled and -roofed, and on either side are circular gravel areas laid out cheaply for car parking and screened by grass mounds and fastigiate tree planting.

The arc of the arena is marked by radial timber-edged steps which rise to the gatehouses; these radial lines emphasize the symmetry of the design. Made from industrial materials, this is an exquisitely simple and economical design (total cost: £270,000) that uses its surroundings rather than rejects them.

A. Hedeland Arena, view from the grass terraces when there was a working gravel pit beyond. It has since closed and the backdrop is now a lake.
B. The terraces with at the top the ticket office, roofed with grass turfs.
C. The arena is set in a heathland landscape marked by gravel workings.
D. The coarse gravel car park, toilet blocks in the foreground, and the area arena beyond, not a place to dress up, although the Opera Hedeland performs here in the summer.

3 Case study Hedeland Arena, Roskilde, Denmark

Human flow and natural change

As stated above, landscape architecture is not purely or even primarily about producing a single, fixed design 'product'. It is about process far more than, say, architectural, car or product design. Landscape designs change and develop over time and as part of wider systems. This process of change is most obvious in a garden or forest, where plants grow, flower and die. Such change inevitably involves uncertainty. No site is isolated. Landscapes develop and change and the way they are experienced is as moving spatial sequences where the observer shifts and the scene changes around them. Landscapes connect with both society and the natural world, and are governed by natural, biological, geological, mechanical and chemical processes as well as by humankind's influence.

Landscape design is about creating spaces through which people variously walk, jog and cycle, as well as in which they sit, play, sun themselves – and observe other people. A garden path can be narrow – a width of 30cm is sufficient to accommodate a walker. A city footpath, by comparison, should be much broader, providing enough space for people to be able to stop, chat and window-shop. Paths in parks may be wider still.

Social activity happens spontaneously when people encounter one another. It might take the form of greetings and conversations, children's play, communal activities from t'ai chi to rounders, cycling, shopping, working or buying a paper from a newsvendor. Creating spaces where such activities can happen is the role of the placemaker. All this social activity requires space. Streets are likewise places of theatre as well as transport routes. The key to successful design for pedestrian movement lies in avoiding unnecessary changes of level or the clutter caused by barriers. As Jan Gehl proclaimed: 'First life, then spaces, then buildings – the other way around never works.'

THE MOVEMENT OF THE LAND
Everything moves eventually. The whole of south-east England is sinking following the retreat of the glaciers. Further north, where the glaciers were actually located, the land is rising for the same reason. In areas of drained peat, the land sinks due to oxidization of the peat. Shrinkable clays crack and subside in the course of dry summers. Both earthquake zones and frozen tundra landscapes can experience sudden changes of level. The lesson of all this is that nearly all land is moving to a degree and landscape design should recognize that, particularly where paving construction is concerned. Rigid construction is one reaction, but that involves laying a concrete base under paving slabs, or using cement mortar in brick walls. This reduces the structure's flexibility, making it more exposed to the stresses of ground movement. Similarly tree roots can disturb and crack walls and buildings and cause paving to rise. The other response is to lay flexible paving, on sand or hardcore. This allows small changes of level, consequent movement can be accommodated and the paving easily relaid.

The character and scale of places change through the seasons and times of the day.

A. Steps in London's Trafalgar Square early in the morning.
B. Steps in Trafalgar Square late in the afternoon being used as a meeting and resting place.
C. Seasonal variation of one of the side avenues at Versailles, Paris, winter.
D. Seasonal variation of one of the side avenues at Versailles, Paris, summer.
E. Daily variation at Trafalgar Square, London, early morning.
F. Daily variation at Trafalgar Square, London, afternoon.
G. Square Jean XXIII, Notre Dame, Paris, late summer.
H. Daily variation at the South Bank, London, early morning.
I. Daily variation at the South Bank, London, afternoon.
J. Square Jean XXIII, Notre Dame, Paris, autumn.

C

D

E

F

G

H

I

J

Marketplace and Waterfront, Odda, Norway

Landscape design for a community space

Located at the head of the extremely long Hardanger Fjord, south-east of Bergen, Odda is a small industrial town of some 7,500 inhabitants best known for its fertiliser plant and zinc production. The town council wished to rejuvenate the quayside, provide for a market and link the east and west sides of town.

Though it's not a particularly pretty town, the views up the fjord, closely embraced by the Hardangervidda mountains, are sublime, and in spring fruit trees blossom along the shore against stirring background views of the ice of the Folgefonna Glacier above. These visual qualities are exploited in Bjørbekk & Lindheim's competition-winning design for a waterfront marketplace.

Bjørbekk & Lindheim have emphasized the marketplace's hard landscape character by focusing on finely detailed grey granite stonework designed by project landscape architect Rune Vik. Planting is limited to a beech (*Fagus sylvatica*) hedge and row of alder trees (*Alnus glutinosa*), which provide a windbreak. The main square is at a corner of the waterside, between two existing buildings. It is paved in granite marked by lighter stripes and crossed by a water runnel fed by a fountain. The runnel leads down some steps into the fjord. Three mast-like poles complete the scene. The eastern section has an oak boardwalk along the water's edge, lined by benches which are protected by timber walls, also in oak, so that you can sit facing the setting sun. This is a classic urban renewal scheme, landscape design acting as a catalyst and providing a focus for an economically challenged town.

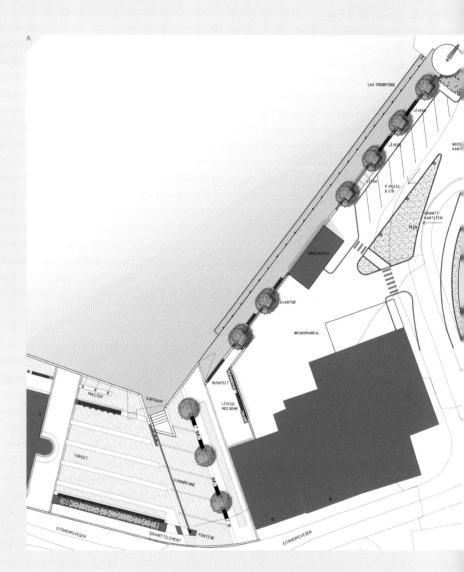

A. Bjørbekk & Lindheim's Odda Marketplace: the plan is simple and minimalistic, with bands of different tones of granite, the detailing is essential to the art. The marketplace is like a stage setting for the people to animate, bringing light and colour into the foreground.

B. The marketplace looks out over the Hardanger Fjord. The fjord is at the rear of the scene, the mountains form the backdrop.

C. Superbly detailed granite stonework.

D. The boardwalk with benches backing onto windbreaks which capture the sun.

E. Odda waterfront consists of a marketplace at the centre of town, with granite paving, a boardwalk, and asphalt surrounds, and constitutes simple and effective place-making.

F. The quayside marketplace, formerly a car park.

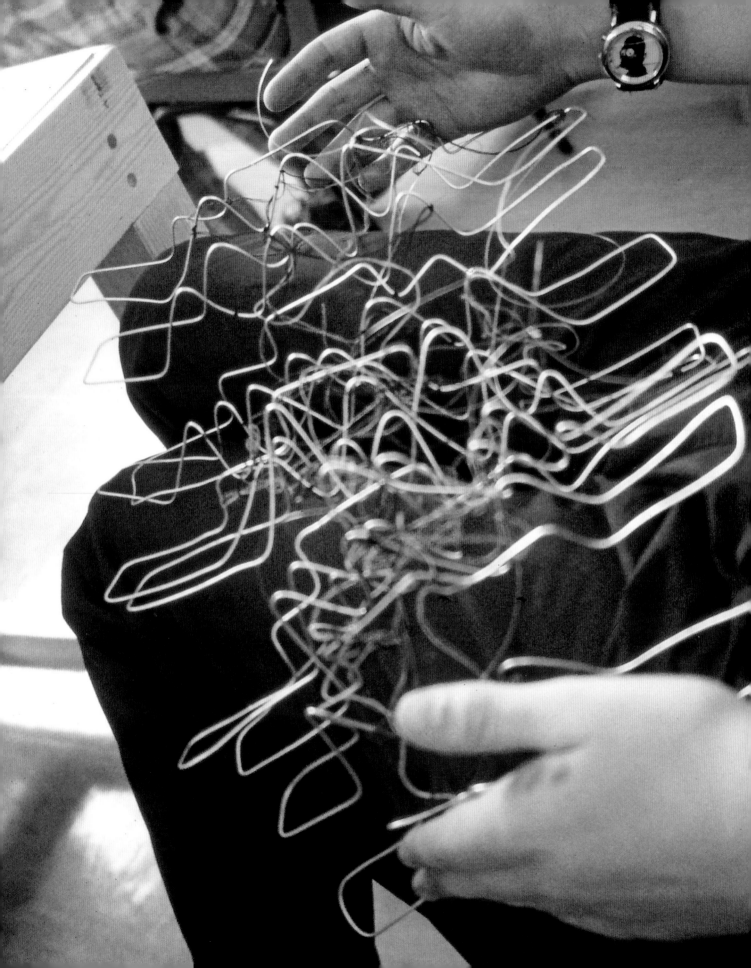

4
Representing the Landscape Design

Simple bent wire 'Linear experiences' model
documenting a journey through the city of London.

The way you represent your design work has a huge impact on its development and reception. Learning how to draw well, for instance, helps you to convey your ideas more effectively to others. This chapter looks at some of the manual and computerized techniques that landscape architects use to represent their designs. We also look at digital data handling such as BIM (Building Information Modelling), and Geographic Information Systems, as well as map making and end with a few words on report writing, because landscape architecture can involve much desk study.

Drawing and sketchbooks

Drawing is a fundamental skill in landscape design: it is how you can test your ideas, record your thoughts and observations, and develop them. Sketching forces you to observe and therefore understand. A photograph is a very different form of record: it can be fleeting, a snapshot, and does not necessarily involve analysis (though of course photography is vital for recording purposes). If you have spent four or five hours drawing an apple tree, on the other hand, you can understand its structure and properties deeply. For the student and the designer, daily sketching – whether in the form of long studies or quick visual notes – is a vital discipline.

A sketchbook can be complemented by a blog and/or digital sketchbook and, supplemented in this way, become a kind of visual diary. Christopher Lloyd was one of the great plantsmen of the twentieth century and recorded his ideas in magazine articles for over 40 years, a practice that enriched and developed his planting design. The blog is a modern equivalent of the old-fashioned daily diary.

The sketchbook is crucial because:

- daily sketching develops discipline. It forces you to see more. It acts as an inspiration and encourages you to develop your design ideas;
- its chronological form encourages personal development and gives you a larger sense of professional direction;
- it permits you to experiment and to consider alternatives;
- it clarifies your thinking and can be used in conversations with other designers in your team;
- it can be mined in the future as an inspiration for other projects, serving as a treasury of design ideas which may not be immediately applicable;
- sketching complements (and can include) writing. A sketchbook can be a place to record new plant names, places to visit and key phrases;
- initial sketch ideas can often be used in formal presentations because a quick sketch may communicate an idea simply and strongly.

Sketchbooks are for experiment in techniques, the resolution of design ideas and the recording of direct observation.

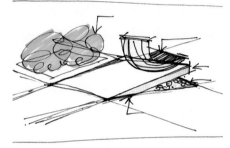

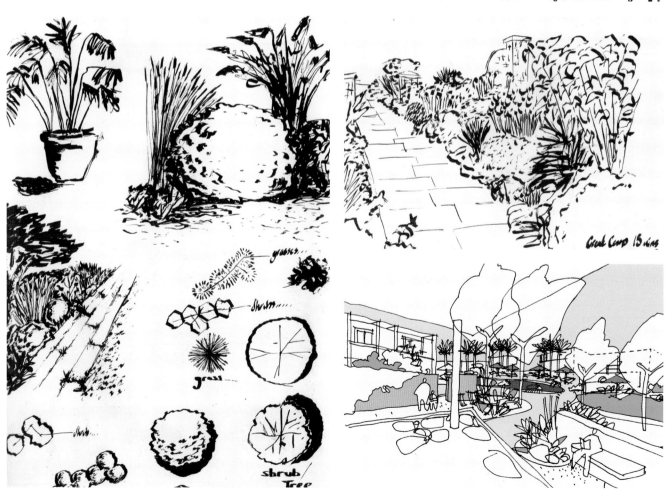

Sketchbook experimentation can include photography, collage, overlay techniques and watercolour rendering.

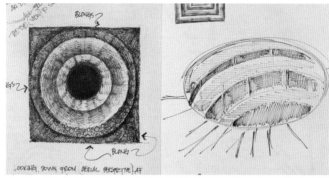

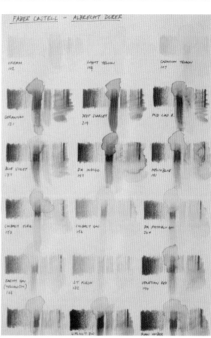

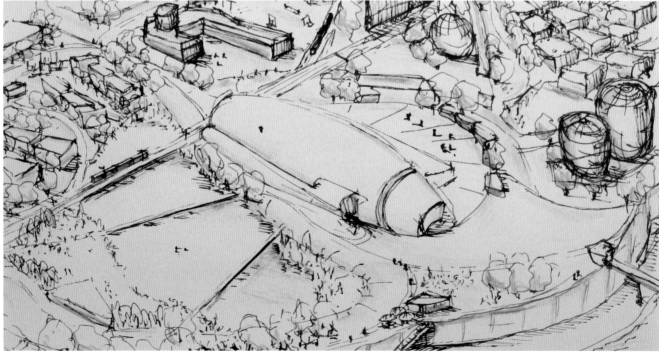

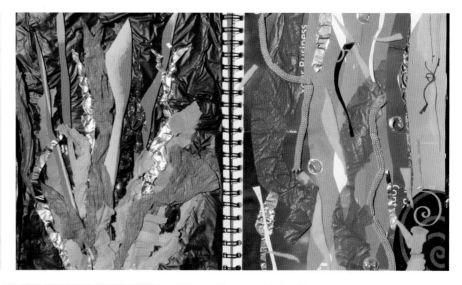

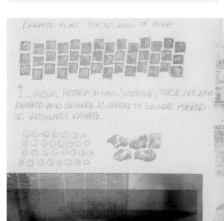

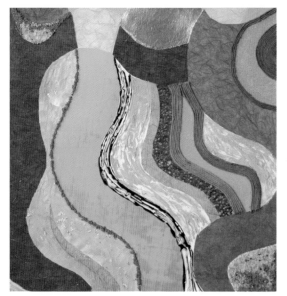

School Courtyard, London

Landscape design for schoolchildren

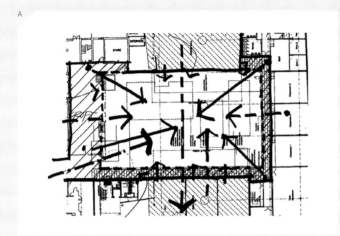

A

A. Spatial organization of the courtyard design starts with the sequence of views out onto the court and the approaches through the building.
B. Orientation, sun and shadow are fundamental to the design of any enclosed space. This sketch identifies the sunny south-facing side and other areas which will be mostly in shade.
C. The design emerges from analysis of the site. Here the designer has proposed 'islands in a sea' or 'mountain tops in cloud' as a metaphor for the design proposal with an informal, asymmetrical design of planting 'islands' emerging from the ground plane, which is the paved circulation area. Metaphor and allegory can be effective ways of expressing a design.
D. This figure describes and justifies the planting, explaining it in terms of shade, vertical connections, range of habitat types and seasonal change.
E. Finally a summary of the meaning of the design is presented in terms of movement (permeability), view from dining room, and ideas of interaction and quieter places of relative solitude.

B

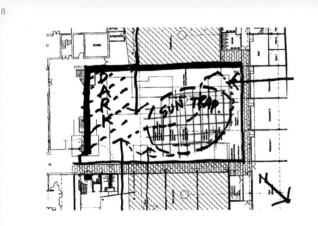

C

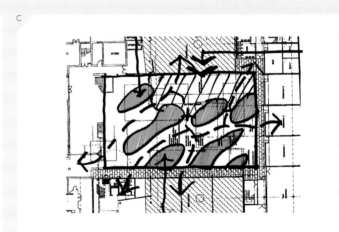

D

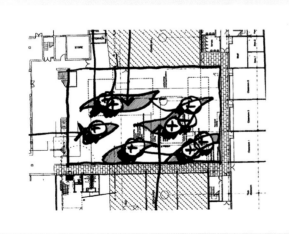

E

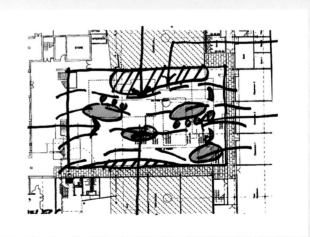

F–H. A courtyard is a simple, enclosed space with strong spatial definition
(the buildings around), and is introverted. It connects with the sky
above and with rooms in the building rather than the outside world.

A. Quick pencil-and-ink sketching techniques.
B. Wet ink on soft paper.
C. Ballpoint pen sketching.
D. Acrylic, mixed media perspective.
E. Cross-hatching used in a traditional pen-and-ink method.

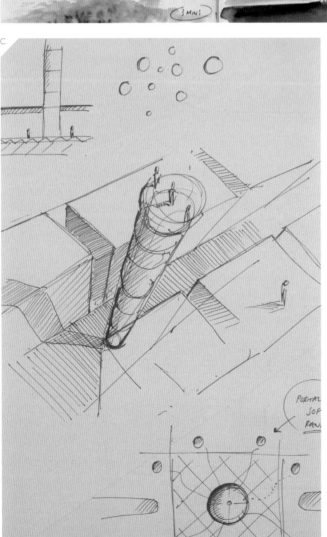

3D modelling and video

Designed landscapes are symphonies of space and form. In theatre design, automobile design and, indeed, the laying-out of Disney theme parks, 3D models serve as the basic design tool. The initial design is produced by modelling, first in rough and then in a more accurate fashion. Designing in two dimensions is by its nature a more distant procedure; 3D modelling allows one to experience a design and begin to travel through it. Such models emphasize the sculptural characteristics of a project: the sculptor Isamu Noguchi, who also designed gardens and landscapes, made beautiful models.

Film, like model work, allows for three-dimensional exploration and so can be of use in landscape architecture. Time-lapse and real-time photography are the most valuable techniques in tracing patterns of movement in urban space. Perhaps their best-known exponent was William H. Whyte, who used film in the 1970s to observe patterns of movement in corporate spaces in New York – something he termed 'people watching'.

Nowadays video is being used in conjunction with physical model-making and digital design programs to produce changing three-dimensional representations of sites, which make it possible to map the effects of development. For a discussion of how digital design can benefit landscape architecture see page 123.

For many designers physical model-making is the best method for exploring spatial concepts.

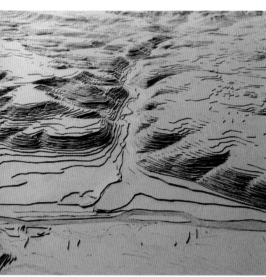

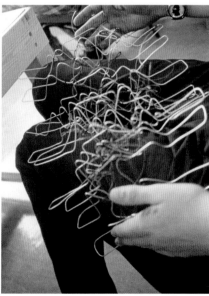

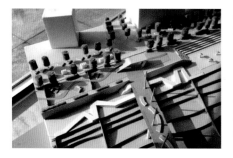

Models are used as development and process tools,
to challenge and document the design intention.

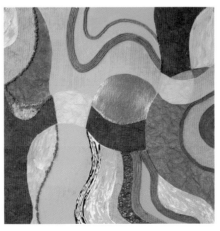

Models can be used to explore both scale and detail in a variety of materials, from early concept to final resolution.

Photography

Photography is an important way of establishing a survey record, particularly in relation to panoramic views and permits an easily accessible, up-to-date office record of a site. Photography can be digitally manipulated to produce before-and-after images, a key aspect in the visualization of the effects of development on an existing site. More often Photoshop is used to produce flat, cut-out representations. But 3D digital design offers better opportunities for producing effective and convincing before-and-after images. Air photography is also useful as a historical record. It dates back to the 1920s.

Sometimes detailed resources survive in obscure sources: one of the authors used the German Army platoon level packs of maps and street photography taken in the 1930s when first working on Moscow projects in 1990.

Before-and-after shots showing the insertion of a new roundabout and road connection for a proposed development.

Digital design

Digital design or Computer-aided Design (CAD), is the standard drawing technique used in offices in the development and construction industry today. Over the last 30 years it has replaced many of the traditional manual (analogue) representation techniques as the preferred method for producing diagrams, orthographic plans, sections, elevations, projections (axonometric and isometric) and perspectives. As a technique, it is highly efficient and editable.

However, to use digital tools and techniques creatively, one must first gain an understanding of the fundamentals of drawing and develop a systematic design process. There are many different ways to accomplish the same task using different kinds of software. Indeed, many software programs directly replicate manual techniques and processes. But often it is still quicker and more natural to use manual rendering and sketching techniques at certain stages of a project. There is also the possibility of creating hybrid representations that combine manual and digital techniques, giving the designer innumerable ways to create non-standard representational forms.

In most offices, the design work follows a pattern using two-dimensional layout drawings initially and, for presentation, 3D model work subsequently rendered in Photoshop. But digital design offers much more than that and comes into its own when it is three-dimensionally based. A 3D design model can be fully explored by the generation of animations and sequences that show both the diurnal and seasonal qualities of the project; it can likewise be used to model time-based predictions in growth and establishment. For design, solid-modelling and animation software (e.g. 3D Studio Max, Rhino, Maya and SketchUp) is increasingly important. These programs, by-products of the computer-games and special-effects industries, allow the fast representation of design ideas.

So what is the primary digital design software for landscape architecture? The choice includes vector-based, raster-based, solid-modelling, video and animation, vector-GIS and raster-GIS software. A true digital design enthusiast would master all six types of program – but, on the downside, this might leave little time to develop expertise in design.

VECTOR-BASED SOFTWARE:
CAD is probably the most widely used landscape graphic software at the present time. AutoCAD, the market leader in its field, originated as a program for architectural drafting and has since developed in many directions. There are bolt-on additions tailored for plumbing designers, circuit designers, structural engineers – and landscape architects. There is also a GIS bolt-on.

Vector graphics are a scalable format composed of individual objects made up of mathematical calculations. Vector images can be resized easily without loss of quality, making them an ideal format for initial design. Vector graphics, however, do tend to have an artificial appearance. They are point-based and the points are joined to produce lines, so in printing vector graphics are known as line-work. Examples of vector graphics formats include Adobe Illustrator (AI), CorelDRAW (CDR), Encapsulated PostScript (EPS), Computer Graphics Metafile (CGM), Windows Metafile (WMF), Drawing Interchange Format (DXF), AutoCAD, other CAD software and Shockwave Flash (SWF).

RASTER-BASED SOFTWARE:
This uses images (e.g. aerial photographs, satellite photographs and textures) and attribute tables. In computer graphics, a raster graphics image, or bitmap, is a data structure representing a generally rectangular grid of pixels or points of colour. Raster images are stored in image files of varying format and are resolution-dependent, in the same way that any photograph will eventually blur as it is enlarged. As such, unlike vector images they cannot be enlarged without loss of quality. Printers describe raster graphics as continuous tones or 'contones'.

A bitmap corresponds bit-for-bit with an image displayed on a screen, generally in the same format. A bitmap is technically characterized by the width and height of the image in pixels and by the number of bits per pixel. Pixel stands for *pix* or picture and *el* or element.

Examples of raster-based software include Painter, Adobe Photoshop, MS Paint and GIMP. For photo-editing work, landscape architects use software such as Photoshop and Photopaint.

Building Information Modelling (BIM)

Traditionally building design has used two-dimensional drawings (plans, elevations, sections, etc.). Building Information Modelling (BIM) goes beyond 3D (width, height and depth) – it also covers geographic information, spatial relationships, shade analysis, and measured quantities and properties of materials (e.g. manufacturers' specifications). This becomes a 'shared knowledge resource' or virtual model of a building or other form of facility. This permits testing of various options during the design and

construction stages – for instance if a civil engineering version of BIM is used it is easy to adjust the vertical profile of a road and investigate the effect on cost or environmental or road safety consequences. BIM is an 'intelligent virtual information model'.

BIM can be applied throughout the lifetime of a facility from design to construction, to operational use and even to eventual demolition and recycling or reuse. The system is handed on from

the design team to the contractor to the operator or building facilities manager. BIM-compatible software includes ArchiCAD, Microstation and Vector Works. The first BIM system was Graphisoft's 'Virtual Building' system introduced in 1987 using ArchiCAD.

During the last three decades CAD has been 'paper-centric', based on producing digital versions of design and construction drawings that previously were produced by hand.

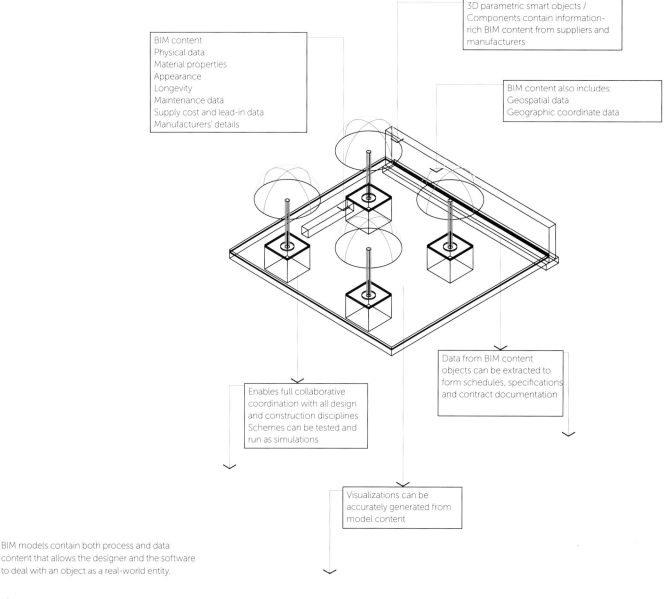

3D parametric smart objects / Components contain information-rich BIM content from suppliers and manufacturers

BIM content
Physical data
Material properties
Appearance
Longevity
Maintenance data
Supply cost and lead-in data
Manufacturers' details

BIM content also includes:
Geospatial data
Geographic coordinate data

Data from BIM content objects can be extracted to form schedules, specifications and contract documentation

Enables full collaborative coordination with all design and construction disciplines Schemes can be tested and run as simulations

Visualizations can be accurately generated from model content

BIM models contain both process and data content that allows the designer and the software to deal with an object as a real-world entity.

Mapping, air photography, satellite imagery and Geographic Information Systems (GIS)

Maps are a key to power. The leading cartographers of the eighteenth century were the French, who mapped their territories in the wake of Louis XIV's great victories. Comprehensive mapping in Britain began after the Jacobite Rebellion of 1745 when the Scottish Highlands were first mapped. This led to the establishment of the British Ordnance Survey, which extended mapping activities first to Ireland and then to the British Empire. George Everest, director of the Great Trigonometrical Survey of India, completed the first triangulation of that country in the 1850s. This was a massive task that took half a century and involved building towers and clearing sightlines through forests.

It has been argued that the American Civil War lasted as long as it did in part because comprehensive mapping of the country's vast territories had not previously been undertaken. It has been suggested that if the terrain had been better understood, the Confederacy might have been defeated more quickly. The need for such maps led to the establishment of the US Geological Survey in 1879.

All landscape architects should have a good knowledge of both mapping and its modern supplements, air photography and satellite imagery. Begin by exploring the NASA website, which offers many views of the world, and also by reviewing the traditional mapping available in the country where you are working. The latter offers the additional advantage of allowing you to explore the recent historical layers of a site. For example, most developed areas of Britain were already mapped at larger scales of 1:1250 by the 1870s. Therefore you can plot the development of docks, roads, mines and quarries and their subsequent use for housing, or shopping centres or nature reserves over the past two centuries.

Datasets are based on topographical mapping. For instance, in the UK the Ordnance Survey offers datasets such as OS Land-Form PROFILE Plus which is based on Ordnance Survey 1:10,000 scale mapping. Note: 1:10,000 map contours are at 5m intervals and are accurate to $\pm$ 1.0m in the countryside and $\pm$ 0.5m in some towns.

However, it is also possible to use global navigation satellite systems or GNSS (sat nav) in mapping and surveying. GPS (Global Positioning Systems) is the best known and is based on US Department of Defense satellite data, but be aware that such data may only be accurate to a few metres, typically $\pm$10m. Nevertheless, use of such satellite-based data is critical in areas with poor topographical mapping coverage such as much of Africa and parts of the Middle East. There is only one other satellite-based global positioning system currently operational, the Russian GLONASS, with others in development in Europe, China, India and Japan. GLONASS is more accurate than GPS at high latitudes (i.e. the polar regions) and low latitudes (i.e. the equator).

The European Union Galileo system may eventually offer the possibility of higher definition and accuracy (to within a metre) when it becomes available. This civilian-based system is designed to be operable with both GPS and GLONASS. The European Space Agency launched the first of the initial four Galileo satellites in October 2011. By 2019 there will be 30 satellites in total; the system is planned to be free for public use.

The Chinese regional navigation system, BeiDou, is scheduled to be extended to cover the Pacific and Asian regions as BeiDou-2 (retitled as Compass) in 2012 and will have a free $\pm$ 1.0m service and a licensed, more accurate service, planned to go global by 2020. In 2012 BeiDou-2 is operating a free service with a $\pm$ 25m accuracy, this will become more accurate as more satellites are launched.

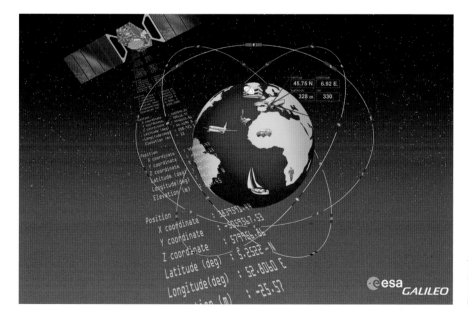

The European Union Galileo global navigation satellite system will offer superior resolution to the US GPS by 2020 while the Chinese BeiDou system is operational now.

GEOGRAPHIC INFORMATION SYSTEMS (GIS)

GIS is a computerized, topographically based dataset first developed in the 1960s in Canada by Dr Roger Tomlinson, a geographer and geologist, for the federal Department of Forestry and Rural Development. This was followed up from 1965 by work at the Laboratory for Computer Graphics at the Harvard Graduate School of Design headed by the architect Howard Fisher. Jack Dangermond, a landscape architect, joined the team in 1967 and aided in developing SYMAP (Synteny Mapping and Analysis Program), which is basically a mapping visualization tool. Later Dangermond set up the GIS software company Environmental Systems Research Institute (ESRI) to further develop GIS. As of 2012, ESRI offers: ArcView, an easy-to-use program; ArcInfo, a more sophisticated program; and ArcGIS, which permits the addition of additional modules to increase functionality. GIS data is expressed as:

- elevation data, either in raster format or vector form such as contours;
- shape layers, which are usually line drawings, for streets, streams, land plot sizes, etc;
- coordinate system descriptions;
- data which describes the shape of the Earth as suggested by the coordinates.

GIS enables interpretation of topographical data, such as mapping or satellite photography data (including ultraviolet photography), but also census and landscape ownership data. It permits a view of the land, and as such is a vital tool for landscape architects as well as for landowners, planning authorities and most government bodies, allowing easy manipulation of information about soils, geology, slope analysis, groundwater and hydrology, vegetation, user preferences, contours, etc. It permits digital manipulation in both two and three dimensions of the sort of layer data that Ian McHarg's students produced by hand in the 1960s at the University of Pennsylvania on plastic overlay sheets. At the macro level it enables landscapes to be interpreted at a regional scale; at the micro level it permits trees to be inventorized and landscape management operations to be recorded and monitored. It also enables landscape architects to produce their own maps.

ZTV (ZONES OF THEORETICAL VISIBILITY)

Analysis of Zones of Visual Influence (or Impact) (ZVI) or Zones of Theoretical Visibility (ZTV) is an objective way of estimating where an object such as a new building will be visible from using computer software with a digital elevation dataset based on topographical contour mapping and spot heights.

The resulting visibility plan shows the potential maximum area of visibility based on the terrain and allows for the screening effect of woods, existing buildings and walls or indeed atmospheric conditions such as mist. ZTVs are part of the Landscape and Visual Impact Assessment (LVIA) which is a component of Environmental Assessment. A full visual assessment is backed up by a site survey to check exact visibility on site.

Software for ZVI analysis is currently either AutoCAD with an add-on such as Key TERRA_FIRMA or GIS software such as Global Mapper.

A

ANALYSING AVERY HILL PARK, LONDON

Historical vs Current Analysis

(Overlaying aerial image with OS Historic Map – 1854 and site boundary shape layer)

— Site boundary

Topographical Analysis

(Derived from DTM/TIN, overlayed with OS colour raster, hillshade analysis and contours)

— Site boundary
— Contour_1m
— Contour_5m

3D Data (ArcScene)

Drape data over elevation raster

Slope degrees
- 0-1
- 2-2
- 3-4
- 5-8
- 9-18

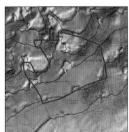

Data Analysis

(Land-use map derived from OS Master map by applying spatial queries to provide additional layers of information)
— Site boundary
▲ Trees 25m from buildings
✳ Coniferous trees
● Culverts
— Water
▨ Trees, scrub
▨ Buildings on site

A. GIS views of Avery Hill Park, London, showing the selective use of various datasets.
B. Example of a 12km-radius, five-point ZTV analysis for a new 64m-high hotel development located at the centre of the circle. The mass of the buildings is most visible from the areas that have the deepest combined colour.
C. Example of a 15km-radius, multi-point, composite radial line ZTV analysis located at the centre of the circle, shown on an Ordnance Survey 1:25,000 map base. The turbine is most visible from the areas that have the deepest blue colour.

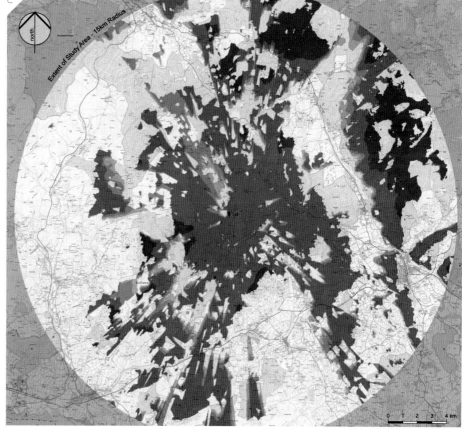

Report writing

Reports are a staple of the design process and report writing is an essential skill for landscape architects and, indeed, all design professionals. A report's aim is to inform as clearly and as briefly as possible. As such it should be written in an appropriately formal and analytical style, be clearly organized (with an introduction, main text and conclusion) and presented, and have been carefully proofread.

A report should generally include the following elements:
- letter of transmittance, describing the purpose and contents of the report, and explaining by whom and when it was commissioned;
- title page;
- table of contents;
- list of abbreviations and/or glossary;
- executive summary/abstract;
- introduction;
- body of text;
- conclusion;
- recommendations for action;
- bibliography;
- appendices.

Presentation and style are important. First impressions count, so consider these simple tips:
- ensure that the separate parts of your report stand out clearly;
- use subheadings;
- use bullet points or numbered points;
- use tables and figures (graphs, illustrations, maps, etc.) for clarification and graphic effect;
- number each page, and usually each clause too, for ease of reference;
- use consistent and appropriate formatting;
- use formal language.

Avoid:
- the inclusion of careless, inaccurate, irrelevant or conflicting data;
- mixing facts and opinions without making a clear distinction between the two;
- unsupported conclusions and recommendations;
- careless presentation and proofreading;
- beginning with negatives.

Landscape and Biodiversity

04 Planting Concept
04.1 Principles
Due to the constrictive nature of the site planting has been focused into three main areas: the lockable enclosed sensory-style experiential gardens, the living roof and the third is the Prince George Road frontage. Each of the garden areas is located to create a natural backdrop to views out of the classrooms and to catch available sunlight to ensure successful establishment, and are seen as explorative resources for small supervised groups of pupils.

Planting is designed to allow clear sightlines for security and supervision.

The development of the planting palette is guided by the school requirements for species that are non-toxic, whether ingested or handled, ideally where possible non-fruiting, non-thorny and free from sharp leaf or stem edges, resilient to damage and easily maintained.

Plants will be selected so any seasonal foliage or flora effects will happen during term time and contain a high proportion of evergreen plants to give a clear planting structure. Planting will be selected to complement the curriculum requirements including their sensory qualities, their ability to attract wildlife, and provide a range of opportunities for a varied learning experience.

The proposed planting palette is comprised of mainly native tree, shrub, groundcover and grass species with a number of naturalized, ornamental and sensory species proposed to enhance visual amenity.

Plant material will be sourced locally.

04.2 Planting palette

TREE SCHEDULE
Latin name
Acer campestre ' Elsrijk'
Acer ginnala
Alnus glutinosa 'Laciniata'
Alnus incana 'Aurea'
Alnus incana 'Laciniata'
Betula albosinensis ' Fascination'
Betula pendula
Betula pubescens
Betula utilis jacquemontii
Carpinus betulus 'Fastigiata'
Liquidambar styraciflua 'Stella'
Pinus sylvestris
Quercus robur 'Fastigiata'
Sorbus aria 'Lutescens'

CLIMBER SCHEDULE
Latin name
Clematis armandii
Clematis vitalba
Hedera hibernica
Hydrangea petiolaris
Jasminum officinale
Lonicera henryi
Lonicera periclymenum
Parthenocissus tricuspidata 'Veitchii'

SHRUB / HERBACEOUS SCHEDULE
Latin name
Acaena buchananii
Acer campestre
Alchemilla mollis
Anemone hupehensis
Astrantia major
Cercidiphyllum japonicum
Cornus alba 'Kesselringii'
Cornus alba ' siberica'
Cornus sanguinea ' Midwinter Fire'
Corylus avellana
Cotinus coggygria 'Flame'
Hamamelis x intermedia 'Diane'
Lavandula angustifolia 'Hidcote'
Miscanthus sinensis
Perovskia atriplicifolia 'Little Spire'
Rosmarinus officinalis
Rosmarinus prostratus
Salix viminalis
Salvia leucantha
Santolina chamaecyparissus
Sarcococca confusa
Sarcococca hookeriana 'Humilis'
Sedum spectabile
Teucrium fruticans 'Azureum'
Verbascum nigrum
Verbena bonariensis
Viburnum x bodnantense 'Dawn'

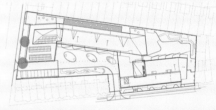
Area of Living Roof

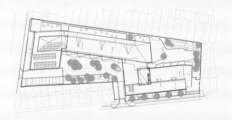
Proposed Tree Planting

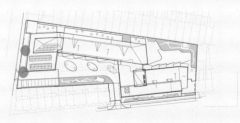
Proposed Shrub Planting

New Horizon SEN School / Full Planning Application- Landscape and Biodiversity   Page 5

Live presentations

As a landscape architect, you will regularly find yourself in the position of having to persuade other people, such as developers and funders, to provide the money to allow you to realize your dreams. This may be as part of an original competitive bidding for a project commission, followed by presentations at design reviews and amplified by public presentations as part of community participation and community design workshops. You will need to convince boards, planning authorities and financiers, not to mention whole communities, that what you are proposing is the best way forward. This requires you to have clear, persuasive ideas and also the capacity to convey them. The ability to stand in front of a committee and argue your case clearly is a critical skill: you have to be able to speak cogently. This is not a context in which you can simply hide behind pretty drawings.

Nowadays most presentations are PowerPoint-based. This is both a blessing and a curse, as it can lead to a condition known colloquially as 'bulletpointitis'. The problem with bullet points, by the way, is that they tend to encourage oversimplification and assertion, and to undermine discourse and explanation. A good presentation planning structure can be abbreviated as PEE (Proposition, Explanation, Evidence).

Therefore (and note that we use bullet points to offer this advice!):

- do show full-screen images and ensure that they actually mean something;
- do not use five images when one will do;
- do use your spoken presentation to explain, enlarge upon and emphasize the points shown on the screen;
- do not read from the screen;
- do face and look at your audience. If you have a lot of listeners, try to catch the eye of five or six individuals distributed through the audience. You will soon notice if they begin to fall asleep;
- don't talk too quickly and be prepared to pause for dramatic effect;
- do practise voice projection – speak, don't shout – and where possible use a microphone (and check with the audience that they can hear at the back).

Public presentation is about confidence, learning how to engage with the audience and to communicate with inspiring clarity.

A. Gare d'Eaux presentation to local councillors and Lille planners, February 2011.
B. Models make presentations easier to explain and easier to understand.
C. Gare St Sauveur Esquisse presentation to City of Lille planners, February 2010.

Villa Garden at Aphrodite Hills, Cyprus

Landscape design for a private garden

This overall plan is for a villa garden design on the Aphrodite resort development in Cyprus. This is the sort of drawing that will be presented to a client together with perspective views and photographs of comparable features, and might often be coloured. The swimming pool is to the right of the villa next to the main terrace. There was prior discussion with the client about how they wished to use the garden, sundeck, cooling pool and entertainment terrace with views to a pavilion.

These ideas were developed further in a more detailed layout plan and the designs were finally completed with a series of computer-drawn plans such as the paving or hardworks plan, showing paving types, patterns, levels, changes of levels, walls and plant beds and any building outlines. These were supported by detailed construction drawings, a planting plan, irrigation and lighting plans and a written specification. The photographs of the construction then show the drawing plan ideas being carried through to the final form, with a line on the plan becoming a line on the ground.

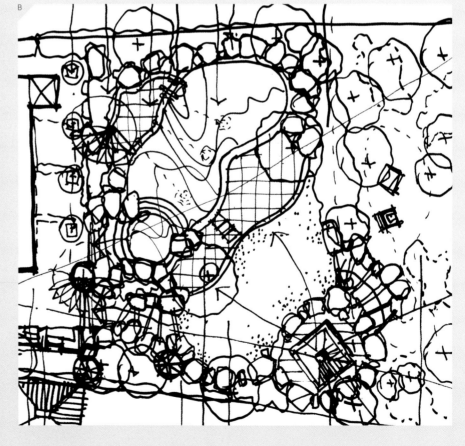

A. Initial felt-pen sketch on tracing paper overscaled site plan, drawn at a client meeting. The drawing mixes analysis graphics with design ideas.
B. Developed initial sketch response for second client discussion meeting in felt pen on tracing paper overlay. The sketch adds composition and form to first ideas but is still informal and was subsequently amended after the meeting. Such informal drawings are quick, involve the client and permit development and change.

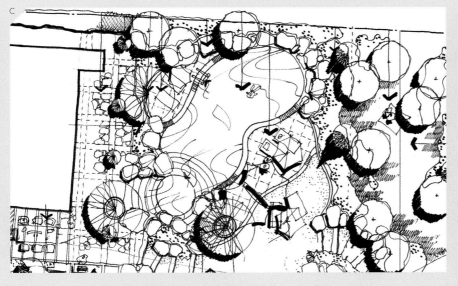

C

C. First presentation drawing detailing the depth of the ideas, drawn on tracing paper using technical wet ink pens and felt and thick marker pens, with shadow and textures added. It was hand-coloured with pencil crayons. Materials and details could be added as notes.
D. Detailed areas begin to be worked up following final client approval: site levels and radii have been added in freehand on the mechanically drawn base and this drawing forms the basis of the final digitally drawn construction package.
E. The final hand-drawn bases are scanned, as black-and-white images, and imported into the CAD software as a background image to a digital line trace drawn in AutoCAD. This forms the basis for hardworks (paving), softworks (planting), lighting and separate pool construction drawings.
F. Construction of a pool: the raw, unfinished freeform concrete structure.
G. The finished pool.

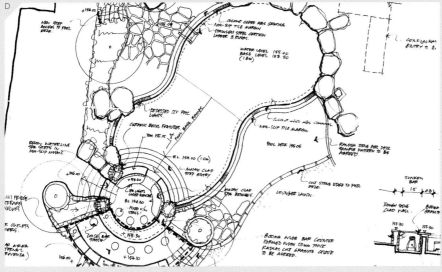

D

F

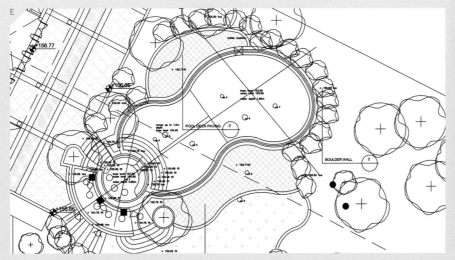

E

G

5
From Design Team to Long-term Landscape Management

View of the Olympic Park, London, showing the wetland area.

The stages of work

Nearly all the development professions such as architecture, engineering and landscape architecture have what are termed 'stages of work', which follow broadly similar models. We have already outlined these in relation to our discussion about fees in chapter 2. To recap, the Landscape Institute's stages of work are as follows:

PRELIMINARY SERVICES
A   Inception
B   Feasibility

STANDARD SERVICES
C   Outline proposals
D   Scheme proposals
E   Detailed proposals
F/G   Production information and bills of quantities
H   Tender action
J   Contract preparation
K   Construction
L   Completion

As it is open to anyone to use other professional bodies' forms of agreement and as it is usual to work on projects led by other professions, we also give the stages of work set out in the Royal Institute of British Architecture (RIBA)'s *Outline Plan of Work* of November 2008, which usefully describes the stages in five main sections:

A/B Preparation
C/D/E Design
F/G/H Pre-construction
J/K Construction
L Use

The *Outline* emphasizes that a project – whether housing development, road or business park – continues after construction work has been completed.

This may be compared with the UK Office of Government Commerce (OGC) guidelines:

1   Business justification (the development professions tend to call this the business case)
2   Procurement strategy
3A   Design brief and concept approval
3B   Detailed design approval
3C   Investment decision
4   Readiness for service
5   Benefit evaluation

This gives another take on how a large client body (central government) sees the development of any capital project in terms of service to the client, whether that is a large school or a warship. So what does this all mean? Here we examine the Landscape Institute's stages of work in detail:

LANDSCAPE INSTITUTE WORK STAGES AND FEES

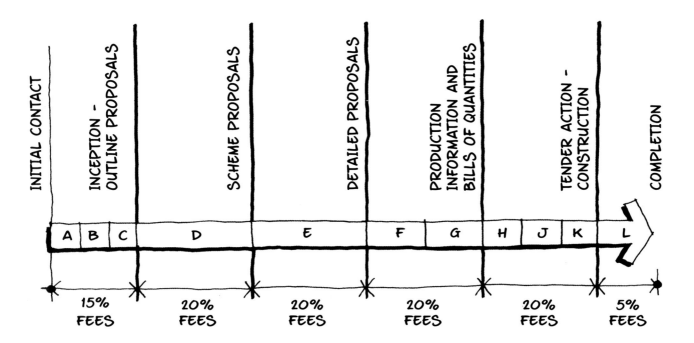

PRELIMINARY SERVICES

A *Inception* covers the client's requirements such as use, timescale and finance are established, and a costed consultancy commission is developed: this is always confirmed in writing at the time. During this period the landscape architect will typically visit the site, obtain from the client information about ownership and any legal restrictions about access and development. Advice regarding other necessary consultants will be given and advice given on any specialist contractors or suppliers advisable (which may require long lead times to organize).

B *Feasibility* involves the testing of the client's requirements, an investigation of alternative solutions to the design, advice on planning applications, and what these may involve. At this stage it will be determined exactly how the standard services are delivered.

STANDARD SERVICES

C *Outline proposals* include development of outline design proposals and meeting with other design consultants to develop the design. Initial meetings with the planning authorities are held to determine their detailed requirements and those of the Construction, Design and Management (CDM) Planning Supervisor.

D *Scheme proposals* involve development of the designs prepared at the outline stage in sketch form

and discussion with other consultants to test their feasibility. Cost estimates are developed, along with the building programme. At this stage the client should be able to agree the direction of the design and the types of materials. There will be continuing discussion with planning authorities leading to a submission of an outline planning application. There will also be discussion with public utility companies and with statutory authorities such as conservation bodies to ensure that the design is acceptable.

E *Detailed proposals* cover development of the designs in sufficient detail to gain the client's approval, coordination of the design with other consultants, and also with suppliers and possible specialist contractors. Costs are tested by obtaining preliminary quotations, a detailed planning application is submitted.

F/G *Production information and bills of quantities* includes completion of 'production drawings' which are final layout plans and construction details, with preparation of a specification (a written document describing the work item by item), schedules (such as planting lists) and advice on preparation of a bill of quantities by the quantity surveyor. A bill of quantities is a list of the items in the works with measured quantities (meaning numbers, areas or linear measurements) of the work which can then be costed by tenderers.

H *Tender action* involves compiling a list of suitable tenderers (i.e. contractors

who can make priced bids for the work), ensuring they can tender at the right time, and then inviting them to submit tenders based on the drawings, specifications and schedules and bills of quantity.

J *Contract preparation* happens as the tenders are submitted. It is based on an agreed, usually standard, form of contract. The contract is signed by both contractor and client and production information (final drawings and details) is provided to the contractor.

K *Construction* can be quite a long period ranging from months to years. During this time the landscape architect will attend site meetings with the contractor and other consultants, monitor the work, advise on site queries, check and certify contractor's accounts and note any changes to the value of the works and advise the client accordingly.

L *Completion* involves checking that the works have been completed as specified and the final account of the contractor under the terms of the contract.

Such a set of stages is an ideal and many variations can be made. For example, at stage H a contract could be negotiated with an approved contractor on the basis of an agreed schedule of prices, rather than let by tender, but this is more common in garden design work than most public or commercial work.

Monitoring paving work on site: landscape architects have to report on whether the construction has been done to specification. If it has, the contractor can be paid.

London 2012 Olympic Park

Teamwork and international practice

One of the key planks for the London 2012 Olympics bid in 2005 was that it would lead to the regeneration of East London. The area along the Lea Valley proposed for the main Olympics Park was a post-industrial wasteland of old railway yards and factory sites, in one of the eight most deprived areas in England.

In 2002 a feasibility study by Insignia Richard Ellis and Arup convinced both the government of Tony Blair and London Mayor, Ken Livingstone, to support the bid. It was the Mayor who pushed for the choice of the Stratford site in East London as the main location for the Olympics.

Following the success of the bid in 2005 landscape architects and economic planners, EDAW, were appointed as masterplanners for the initial stage. EDAW was a large, international environmental design and planning firm with an HQ in San Francisco. Founded originally in 1939 by Garret Eckbo and Edward Williams, two of the heroes of West Coast Modernism, the firm has been owned since 2005 by AECOM, a large development consultancy conglomerate. This is the extreme end of global corporate landscape practice. EDAW had worked previously on the 1976 Montreal Olympics and on the Sydney Olympics Village of 2000 and on the Aquatic Park for the 2008 Beijing Olympics. In 2006 their President was English landscape architect Jason Prior. EDAW undertook the initial masterplanning. Later AECOM were to win the project for the masterplanning of the 120ha Rio de Janeiro 2016 Olympics Park in Barra de Tijuca.

In 2006 the Olympics Development Authority was set up to oversee the commissioning of the design and construction contracts for the Olympics. Their head landscape architect was John Hopkins and he oversaw the international design competition in 2008 for the 250ha Olympic Park and its legacy which was won by US landscape architects George Hargreaves with English firm LDA as executive landscape architect. However, the execution of all the work involved a significant proportion of the English landscape profession, with garden designer Sarah Price designing the framework of the gardens and University of Sheffield professors James Hitchmough and Nigel Dunnett designing the meadow and herbaceous planting displays along the River Lea. Engineers Atkins led the reclamation and Arup undertook the river engineering.

The Olympic Park housed the main 80,000-seat stadium, tennis and archery, velodrome, hockey, handball and the swimming centre as well as the Olympic Village. Many of these facilities will be retained and the Olympics Village will become permanent apartment housing.

The London Legacy Development Corporation was set up from 1 April 2012 by the Mayor of London to develop the permanent park of 226ha as well as the Thames Gateway and their in-house landscape architect is Phil Askew. In August 2012 Land Use Consultants were commissioned to design the northern section and James Corner Field Operations of New York to design the southern section. The Olympic Park reopened to the public as a permanent park for East London as the Queen Elizabeth II Park in July 2013.

A. The 2012 Olympics were about architectural display set in a planted setting; the bridges were built extra wide for 2012 and narrowed for the legacy park.

A

B

B. The waterways were bordered by
planted promenades.
C. The Olympic Stadium viewed from the planted
Greenway.
D. The wetland meadow, planted with fast-growing
tree species, begins to create an informal
parkland structure.
E. The stadium to the left, Anish Kapoor's red
Orbit viewing tower and, across Waterworks
River, the Water Polo Arena.

C

D

E

Multi-disciplinary design teams

An individual commission may require the creation of a team with each member or practice representing a different but necessary skill: for example, in competition submissions, when an architect or engineer needs the help of a landscape designer. The landscape architect would join the team for that specific commission. For competitions, this will usually be on a speculative basis. If a firm commission is forthcoming, it is important to negotiate a fee and working agreement that properly cover your input. To do this, you need to forecast the workload in terms of deliverables, e.g. drawings and the time it will take to produce them. A quick rule of thumb is to calculate the estimated number of days per formal drawing: it can take ten days to produce a drawing (if you include the meetings and time to attend design meetings and liaise with other consultants). This then allows you to calculate an appropriate time fee. Alternatively a percentage fee might be calculated, based on the estimated capital cost of the work.

For collaboration with other professions to be effective, areas of competence and ways of working have to be clearly established. The most common members of an engineering or architectural development project design team include the following:

Engineers may be structural engineers (responsible for the structural design of buildings or bridges), civil engineers (responsible for roads), or mechanical and electrical engineers (electricity, water and other services). Specialist engineers may also be required for high-voltage overhead electrical lines or underground work.

The quantity surveyor (or QS) is a type of cost advisor found specifically in the UK and Commonwealth countries. Other territories have cost engineers, but sometimes costing and measurement are undertaken in-house by the designers.

Project managers (often quantity surveyors) are a fairly recent development and

plan, organize and direct the overall resources of the project – especially the design resources.

Development surveyors advise on assembling land and its subsequent development, usually with the support of letting agents. Letting agents deal specifically with the marketing and letting of a speculative commercial project such as an office block or business park.

Planning consultants may well be required at the pre-planning permission stage. Teams might also include other specialists such as archaeological or ecological

consultants, forestry or agricultural advisors, soils or geotechnical consultants and economic planners.

Project management requires clear lines of communication and structure of responsibilities. The following questions need to be addressed from the outset:

- **When?** Phases and milestones.
- **How much?** Capital costs, fees and ongoing revenue and management costs.
- **Why?** Goals and objectives.
- **What?** Outcomes and deliverables.
- **How?** Processes and tasks.
- **Who?** Roles, responsibilities and deliverables.
- **With what risk?** Risks and trade-offs.

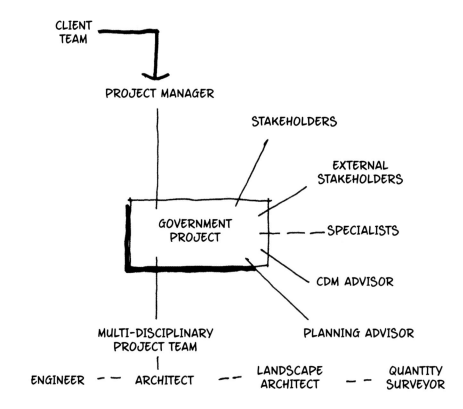

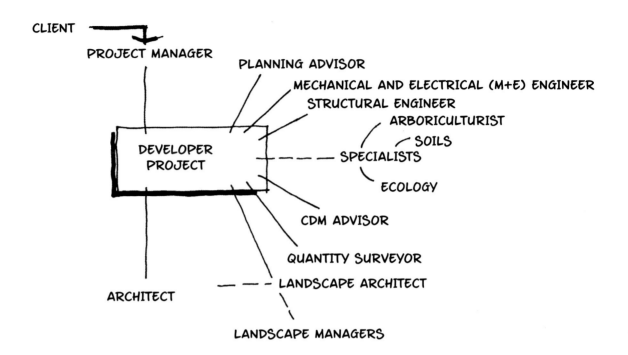

CLIENT → PROJECT MANAGER

PLANNING ADVISOR

MECHANICAL AND ELECTRICAL (M+E) ENGINEER

STRUCTURAL ENGINEER

ARBORICULTURIST

SOILS

SPECIALISTS

ECOLOGY

DEVELOPER PROJECT

CDM ADVISOR

QUANTITY SURVEYOR

LANDSCAPE ARCHITECT

ARCHITECT

LANDSCAPE MANAGERS

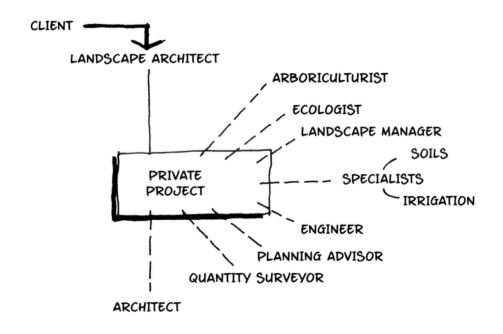

CLIENT → LANDSCAPE ARCHITECT

ARBORICULTURIST

ECOLOGIST

LANDSCAPE MANAGER

SOILS

SPECIALISTS

IRRIGATION

PRIVATE PROJECT

ENGINEER

PLANNING ADVISOR

QUANTITY SURVEYOR

ARCHITECT

The programme of work and the design team

Initially it will be necessary to determine how the design team is to operate, There should be a lead consultant – perhaps the consultant who is responsible for the biggest cost element of the work: e.g. the dam engineer for a reservoir project, the architect for a building – or a specialist project manager.

The overall programme of design production work should be established, usually in bar-chart form showing delivery dates for each consultant. There will be formal design team meetings, typically weekly or fortnightly, at which progress is reviewed, current designs are presented to the whole team, and design issues are discussed and decided. It is vital that these be quickly and clearly minuted.

Sometimes the design team might be led by a planner in the early stages leading up to the submission of a successful planning application. Afterwards, the lead project consultant will take over for the detailed design stage and the production drawings.

Design team meetings might be attended by the client or their representative. But there may be additional project meetings with cost advisors, letting agents and outside funders (often banks or charities) as well as the client.

In an ideal world, the brief should fix the extent of the project at the outset but this is rarely what actually happens. Project team meetings should record any changes made to the original brief in the form of change orders.

A change order is an agreed description of work to be added to (or removed from) the original scope of work set out in the design contract, and which therefore amends the original contract value or completion date. Cuts in the capital value of a project invariably involve additional expenditure on design fees since designs have to be redesigned and drawings have to be redrawn.

in the outline programme tasks are represented in chronological order

TASK
- ◆ 1) CONSULTANTS APPOINTMENT
- ● 2) WORK STAGE A- INCEPTION
- ● 3) WORK STAGE B- FEASIBILITY
- ◆ 4) STAGE B CLIENT PRESENTATION
- ● 5) WORK STAGE C- CONCEPT DESIGN
- ◆ 6) STAGE C- CLIENT PRESENTATION
- ● 7) WORK STAGE D- DESIGN DEVELOPMENT
- ◆ 8) STAGE D CLIENT PRESENTATION AND APPROVAL
- ◆ 9) PLANNING APPLICATION SUBMITTAL
- ● 10) WORK STAGE E- TECHNICAL DESIGN
- ◆ 11) STAGE E CLIENT APPROVAL
- ● 12) WORK STAGES F/G- PRODUCTION INFORMATION
- ● 13) WORK STAGE H- TENDER ACTION
- ● 14) WORK STAGE J- MOBILIZATION
- ◆ 15) START ON SITE
- ● 16) WORK STAGE K- CONSTRUCTION ON SITE
- ◆ 17) PRACTICAL COMPLETION
- ● 18) WORK STAGE L- POST PRACTICAL COMPLETION
- ◆ 19) HANDOVER
- ● 20) MAINTENANCE PERIOD

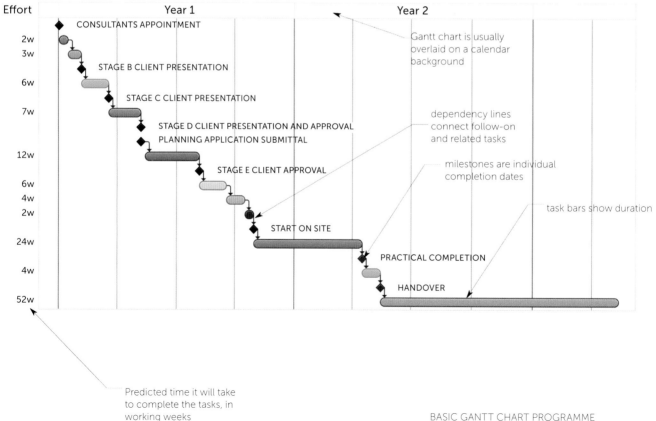

BASIC GANTT CHART PROGRAMME

Costing a project

Adequate cost planning is critical to any project and should be discussed from the outset. This is especially so in the case of landscape architecture, where costing by cost planners or quantity surveyors is often not comprehensive and may prove inadequate. There are two aspects of costing: capital costs and ongoing maintenance and management. Many landscape architects tend to avoid thinking about maintenance costs but it's an essential consideration to ensure that proposals prove fit for purpose in the long run. The reason why so many public fountains are dry is that the cost of maintaining them was not considered in the initial planning stage and the financial arrangements to support those costs were not set up.

Main considerations to establish early on are:

- an adequate cost estimate and design programme – the timetable for the production of the designs and drawings, for costing purposes and then for a planning application and finally for production information (e.g. working drawings) so that contractors can tender for the work;
- tender programme – the timetable for competitive tendering – this requires the selection of suitable companies, a reasonable time period for tendering and then time to consider and check the tenders and appoint a successful contractor;
- site programme – the programme of works with effective and realistic timescales attached covering all work up to completion;
- maintenance programme and responsibilities and financing.

In this section we discuss in particular the costs of public parks because they are the 'purest' kind of project a landscape architect is likely to be responsible for, in the sense that their main *raison d'être* is the designed landscape. However, the sorts of cost analysis necessary in planning a public park can be applied to all built projects.

Four interrelated questions should be asked at the inception of any park project, which are (in no particular order):

- What is the capital cost?
- What is the ongoing maintenance cost?
- How are the capital and maintenance costs to be funded?
- What is the park for?

There is no point in embarking on the large capital investment that a park requires without considering its future management and its finance. One way to fund maintenance and support a park is to tap into the increase in the value of the adjacent land consequent on the project. This has been a historically successful model, illustrated by the example of Regent's Park in London, which is part of the Regent Street development by John Nash and belongs to the Crown Estate. Service charges on the buildings fund maintenance and management. Compare Victoria Park in East London, where finding adequate funding for its maintenance is a continuing challenge.

Parks should be integrated into transport and real-estate developments. The mantra should be: transport + parks + sound long-term management = successful long-term real-estate investment = good community development. Enhanced land values can be equated with good community and ecological development, fundamental *desiderata* of most forms of urban development. The Emscher Park is an illustration of this on a grand scale (see p.44).

On page 144 is a survey of landscape capital costs for various West European parks, which illustrates how to undertake initial cost estimating based on the land area and type or complexity (and therefore cost) of a project. Outline costing should be based on precedent.

The private-sector benefits consequent on transport and environmental improvements should be tapped in order to fund public parks. Alternatively park developers should keep control of the freehold of development land around a new park so that profits and service charges go into the public purse and help to fund the park. This is not a new concept: it is common practice in business-park development.

Transport + parks + sound, long-term investment = Successful long-term real-estate investment = Good community development

PROJECT COSTS

Project costs diagram for a typical park development, including design time and fees can equate to up to 10 per cent of the development programme. The ongoing annual maintenance and management costs should be identified at the project inception.

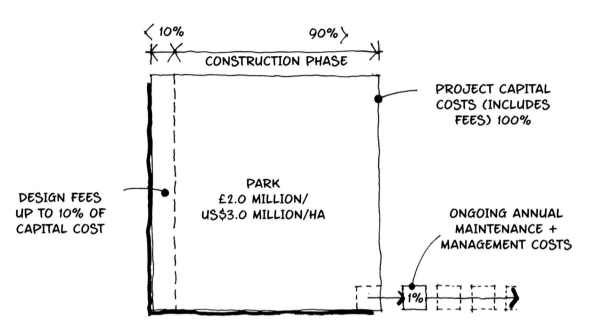

CONTRACT DOCUMENTS

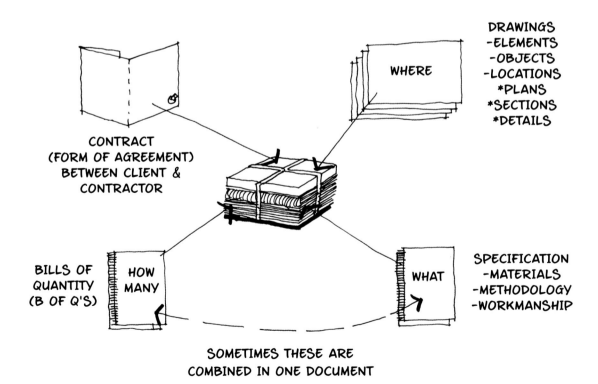

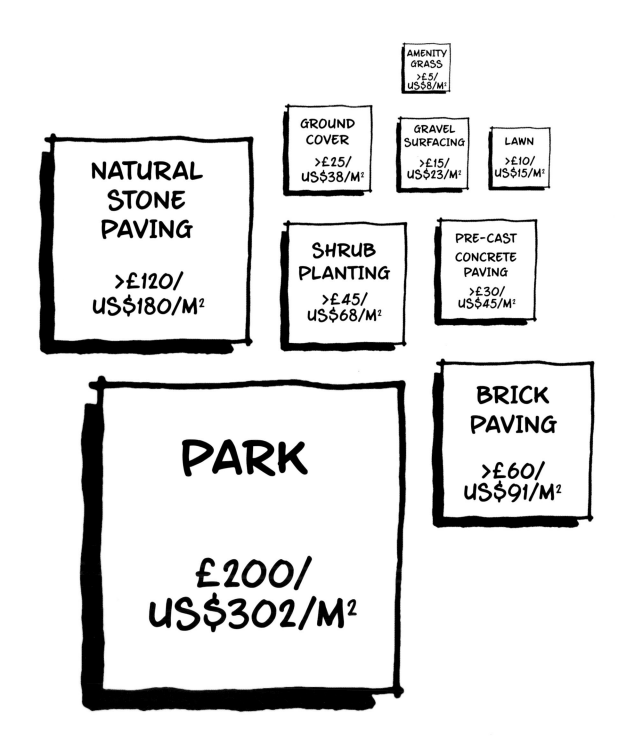

The finance required for landscaping a park depends on the sort of park that is being created. If it's an intensive urban city centre park, then that would equate to over £300/m². If it's a parkland effect, along the lines of the Riemer Park in Munich or the Thames Barrier Park in London, then around £100–200/m² (allowing for remediation to a certain standard) might be reasonable. A cheaper approach, like that adopted at Duisburg Nord near Essen or the Centre for Alternative Technology (CAT) in Wales, might employ natural regeneration or forestry techniques with limited areas of intensive use.

Parks require functions that attract users. This was one reason for the success of the Parc de la Villette in Paris, where the presence of the national science museum ensures about five million visitors per annum. Lack of a sufficient attraction led to the failure of the Earth Centre near Doncaster, UK. The Parc de Bercy in Paris works well because it is in the centre of a redevelopment area (*Zone d'Aménagement Concerté* or ZAC). It thus draws in the local residential population as well as attracting a wider range of visitors owing to the presence of upmarket shopping and cafés and a related entertainment centre. It has also fostered good community and school relations: local primary schools have vegetable plots. A park is not automatically an attraction *per se* – many suburban parks are underutilized because of lack of investment in their care and management. A successful park can always become unsuccessful if management strategies are poor.

Successful and effective parks vary greatly in finance and cost structure. Generally the French and US examples cost more than recent British examples. For instance, the Thames Barrier Park including remediation at £151 per m² was just above one-third of the costs per m² of the Citröen-Cévennes in Paris at €651/m². Both were developed on former industrial sites, using the same designer, Allain Provost. The difference in cost is reflected in the intensity of facilities which is subsequently seen in the different intensities of use: if you pay more, you tend to get more.

Lower-cost parks are possible, but either offer less intensity of use and/or require an approach to remediation that aims to control rather than to remove on-site toxicity. The German practice is to allow vegetation to develop over time, naturally, which can require the exclusion of the public for decades; it also requires an acceptance of low-intensity use (because there will be less paving or expensive features) once the park is opened linked with active management as at Duisburg Nord and the other large German post-industrial parks.

What is the cost of a city park? Asking this question begs the further question: What is a city park? The projects surveyed by cost at end of 2011 prices per m² can be grouped as follows:

A >£200/m²
High-cost, intensive-use urban parks with a high proportion of paving, structures and water features, large numbers of buildings and high levels of intensive horticulture requiring high-quality management: e.g. Paris parks or the two Chicago examples, the Millennium Park and Lakeshore East.

B £100–200/m²
Medium-cost parks such as the Thames Barrier Park in London, the Bordeaux Botanic Garden or the Westergasfabriek Park in Amsterdam, involving intensive-use spaces and high-level maintenance but tending to be less ambitious than the parks in group A.

C £50–100/m²
Low-cost parks of various types, with forestry and parkland developments usually involving extensive grassland. Examples include the Parc Diagonal Mar, Barcelona, or Rotten Row Gardens, Glasgow.

D <£50/m²
Very low-cost parks, with forestry and simple designs, phased developments, developments involving ruderal growth (natural regeneration) such as Duisburg Nord Landschaftspark and some involving volunteer or low-cost labour such as CAT in Wales.

E *Garden festivals*
In Britain, garden festivals were developed at two-yearly intervals from 1984 to 1992 and were intensively developed large parks which opened for six months with millions of visitors, They were developed on derelict land and given the lack of large-scale park design in Britain in the last 60 years they are comparable to large parks. They ranged in cost from £78/m² at Liverpool to £350/m² at Glasgow (at inflation updated 2011 prices).

A. Centre for Alternative Technology (CAT), a post-industrial site, developed by a charity on a long-term, low-cost basis at £30/m².
B. Earth Centre, Doncaster, the phase 1 costs worked out very low, at £35/m², but this development ultimately failed because it could not attract planned further capital funding and National Lottery grants.
C. Duisburg Nord Landschaftspark, also on an industrial site, was low cost at £24/m² because the fundamental idea was to encourage natural regeneration of vegetation.
D&E. Centre for Alternative Technology (CAT), Machynlleth, Wales succeeded because it grew incrementally on a low-cost basis.
F. Duisburg Nord Landschaftspark.
G. Green roof at CAT, built with low-cost, on-site materials not expensive proprietary systems.

A

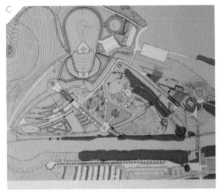

A. Thames Barrier Park, a development on derelict land. Remediation costs tend to be high, but overall costs here were low at £151/m^2.

B. Centre for Alternative Technology, Machynlleth, Wales: Walter Segal-inspired buildings based on minimum cutting of standard building materials such as timber or panels and the use of compost from the site to raise soil productivity.

C. Plan of the Earth Centre, Doncaster.

D. Earth Centre, Doncaster, here the old coal colliery site had been reclaimed before the development began and so everything had to be built from scratch.

E&F. Duisburg Nord Landschaftspark, largely a conservation project, it was low cost, involving managed access to the steelworks structure but leaving old railway yards to vegetate naturally.

Landscape management

All landscape architects should have an understanding of landscape management, which relates to what happens to a site after the initial development work has been completed. Much more so than, say, in architecture, where the architect hands over work that is essentially finished. In landscape architecture handover (technically 'practical completion') is a crucial – and open-ended – stage of any landscape architecture project and should be planned and costed accordingly. For instance, it does not make sense to spend, say, £2,000 on a large street tree and then not put in place an arrangement whereby the stakes are checked regularly to ensure that they are not rubbing against the side of the tree so that the bark is wounded and fungal rot sets in. Too often the result is a dead tree within a few years.

The source of future financing should be determined as early as possible. A good example of how not to do this was provided by the London Docklands Development Corporation (LDDC) in the period 1980–97. In the first place, it ignored the critical importance of both good infrastructure development, especially public transport, and open space in leading environmental and then economic urban development. It also refused to consider what would happen when the Development Corporation was disbanded – hence not only the saga of the Thames Barrier Park (see p.74) but the more general problem of how to fund public-realm maintenance including roads, parks and open spaces.

By contrast German Garden Festivals (*Bundesgartenschauen*) have always included planning for their long-term after-use, generally using public sector funding. The first was held in Hanover in 1951; the site is now the 21ha Stadtpark. One of the latest garden festivals is that in Koblenz in 2011 which was 48ha and drew over 3.5 million visitors.

The 102ha Queen Elizabeth II Park, site of the 2012 Olympics, is being developed by the London Legacy Development Corporation. It aims for nine million visitors per annum (slightly more than the Parc de la Villette's seven million annual visitors). Contracts are to be let for landscape maintenance. However, it remains to be seen whether the long-term management will remain with the Mayor of London or become the responsibility of the Royal Parks, a central government agency with public-sector funding.

LANDSCAPE MANAGEMENT

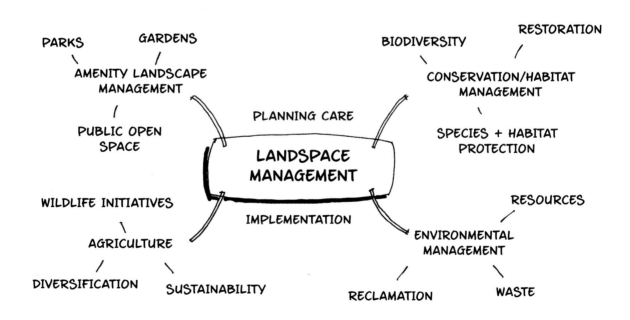

The Parks Trust, Milton Keynes, UK

Long-term management by a community charity

Milton Keynes, 'last and largest of the English New Towns', has a population of 195,000 and covers 2,119,900ha including 190km of cycleways, a 120km-long highway system with generous roadside planting, 1,800ha of linear parks, and the 20 million trees of what was intended to be a 'forest city'. Set up in 1992, the Parks Trust was endowed with a portfolio of commercial properties (offices, shops and industrial property, pubs, hotels and a watersports club) in order to fund the open-space management.

The Trust's key role is stewardship. There are 325ha of parkland pasture grazed by sheep and cattle, 57 horse paddocks, 121 ponds, three ancient woodlands – one an SSSI (Site of Special Scientific Interest) – and 160ha of lakes. The Trust spends £4 million annually on public open-space management and plants around 100 trees and shrubs daily (tens of thousands every year to achieve its aim of producing a forest city). It also has a school and pre-school and adult education programmes run by four coordinators.

The original planting was at high densities to give early effect and a continuing programme of thinning and total removal of fast-growing poplar and willow trees was always planned. There is limited use of herbicides and a regular programme of stream and river dredging to prevent them becoming clogged with vegetation.

The maintenance work is overseen by a small operations team, who supervise landscape maintenance contracts and improvement works – landscape contractors carry out most of the maintenance operations. This work includes grass cutting, weed control, shrub pruning, hedge cutting, coppicing and treework, leisure route resurfacing and litter collection. The Parks Trust has established a horticultural apprentice scheme and in 2010 employed 35 local landscape contractors, who in turn employ a further 200 people.

All this activity continues at no cost to Milton Keynes City Council, the revenue for the charitable trust comes from their property and investment assets.

This 2011 statement of the Trust's key values is worth quoting.

1. Excellence
We demonstrate a commitment to high standards in all that we do, provide leadership in our field and strive for success by being professional, innovative and creative.

2. Integrity
We believe in being open, forthright and honest in our dealings with people and organizations and in adopting behaviour consistent with our values.

3. Collaboration
We work with others for the greater good of the community, cultivate long-term relationships and partnerships, and respond to the needs of local people and organisations.

4. Valuing people
We aim to treat everyone with respect. We are committed to the development of all our people, paid and volunteers, including the fulfilment of potential and the recognition and celebration of achievement.

5. Responsibility
Our stewardship involves: safeguarding the environment for future generations; being accountable for all that we do, including the consequences of any decisions we take; and making the best use of all our resources.

A. Milton Keynes main distributor road.
B. Milton Keynes is a sea of single species block planting, here cotoneaster and laurel surround the Willen's Lake car park.
C. Willen's Lake, Milton Keynes, a successful balancing of a stormwater and a recreational facility. It was created in 1972–74.

In London's Docklands it was the private sector that believed in masterplanning and a quality environment in the short and long term. So the Reichmann Brothers' development of Canary Wharf included a costing for maintenance from the very beginning. The service charge required to provide an adequate public-realm maintenance regime amounts to only a few pence per square metre. The challenge for public-sector planners is to ensure such a revenue stream is established from the beginning. This can be done by planning process and often long-term developers (as opposed to speculative developers) will wish to do so from the beginning. The large London landed estates such as the Grosvenor Estate (which owns much of Mayfair), the Bedford Estate (Bloomsbury), the Crown Estate (Regent Street and Regent's Park) and the Eton Estate (Primrose Hill) are examples of long-term urban developers.

Two sectors of the economy where land-management costs are provided for from the start are forestry (where a 50–100-year timescale is not unusual) and agriculture, but both make a tangible financial return on their investments. The equivalent in the private sector is the business park, where an enhanced environment leads to a sustainable economic return in the form of rental value being maintained or increased. That is also why many private-sector housing-estate developers stress the enhanced value that a maintained environment can produce.

One good precedent for financing of long-term management and maintenance is provided by the National Trust of England and Wales. This is a charity that exists to maintain the historical and natural heritage 'in perpetuity'; in consequence, when accepting new land, it always requires an endowment (often in the form of surrounding agricultural land but sometimes in the form of a fund) to continue to support that heritage. The National Trust is now one of the largest landowners in the UK.

Park and garden maintenance requires planning. The location of the maintenance depot should ideally be central. The tendency of some landscape architects is either to forget the maintenance depot until late in the masterplanning process or to initially hide it away on the periphery. If propagation of plants is to be on-site then the greenhouses and holding areas should also be designed and of course there should be secure buildings to store machinery and chemicals. Security concerns, though important, need not mean that the maintenance depot and greenhouses are hidden away. The nurseries and greenhouses of many National Trust properties, for instance, are accessible to the public.

Many privately owned 'public spaces' in London are high-pressure hose-treated on a daily basis in order to keep the paving pristine and remove chewing gum. While it is admirable that the necessary finance has been put in place, it is questionable on sustainability grounds whether this is a wise way to use drinking water – London only has the one potable (drinking) water supply system. In Paris, by contrast, irrigation water in parks is taken from a separate non-potable water supply.

The Netherlands has led the way in not using pesticides in public parks and open spaces. The scheme began in Arnhem in 1984 in perhaps difficult circumstances since the decision to go over to a non-pesticide maintenance system was made more or less overnight on political grounds. Non-pesticide-based management requires a workforce trained in such techniques and also requires public acceptance of the difference in results: one man's *Taraxacum officinale* is another man's weed (*Taraxacum* is dandelion).

A. Canary Wharf,
B. High-pressure hose treatment using drinking water is wasteful of a scarce resource, example at Canary Wharf, London.
C. Wageningen, the Netherlands: meadow grass on roadside verges, managed without pesticides.

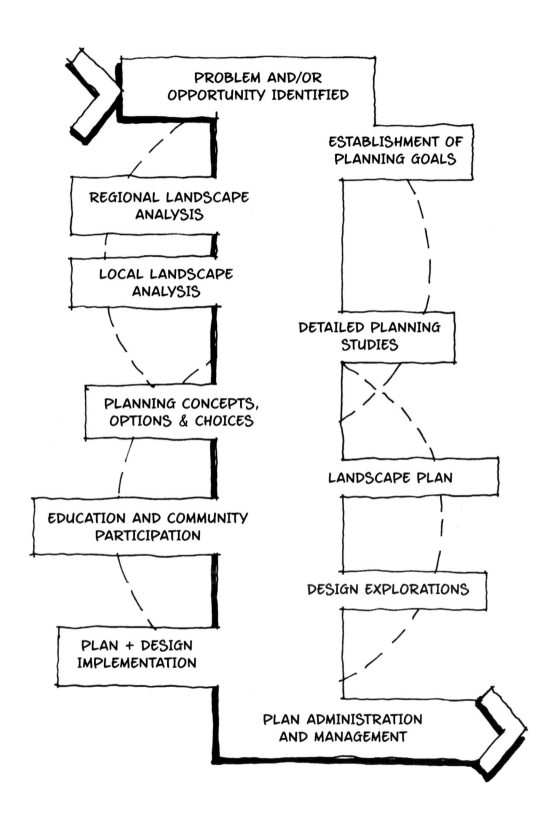

Dr Jac. P. Thijssepark, Amstelveen, the Netherlands

A public park intensively maintained

Amstelveen, a relatively small suburban town on the edge of Amsterdam, has a policy of integrating green areas with housing, and has 16 such *heemparken* or *heemgroenen* (there are about 170 in the Netherlands as a whole). Management is key to the ongoing success of these parks. Their design today is largely the product of evolving plant communities based on management practices.

Jacobus Pieter Thijsse (1865–1945) was a Dutch schoolteacher and nature conservationist who wrote many books including both floral and ornithological guides. He was instrumental in setting up several nature conservation organizations and was the 'father of the Dutch ecological movement'. In 1925 Thijsse established a 2ha public demonstration garden in Bloemendaal, Thijsse Hof, representing the habitat types of the Kennemerland dunes. This was designed by the park architect Leonard Springer (1855–1940).

Begun in 1940, the Thijssepark was the first larger park designed according to the principle of representing a natural habitat flora by planting in easily identifiable groups of plants. The Thijssepark was the first *heempark* in the Netherlands – C.P. Broerse (1902–95), the park's landscape architect, coined the term in 1946.

The design consists of a series of spaces enclosed by tree and taller shrub planting with views from one to another, and it runs alongside the Hoornsloot polder (a wide polder canal). The skill in the planting design and its maintenance is in the selection of indigenous plants. The planting species are characteristic of native peat vegetation and organized for educational display, so there is one-species block planting. Trees are thinned from time to time to ensure that light reaches the ground layer of vegetation.

The layout is in a free, Romantic style, with a series of interconnected spaces of varying size interspersed with pools and channels; the composition is formed by the plants. Paths wind sinuously and create different views; the trees and higher shrubs form screens allowing unfolding views as one walks through woodland from one space to the next. Because of the composition of spaces and the planting design, the park appears much more extensive than it actually is (the area is only 5.3ha, with a width of just 50–100m for the most part). Playing with space in this way is a characteristic garden effect.

Paths are laid in gravel over a bound base with no visible edging and a small-diameter topping course. Precast concrete stepping stones, 400 x 400mm, are used with a large, exposed aggregate. Pools are edged in the east with timber planks and in the west with large-diameter tree trunks. The water is standing water, as is usual in a polder (so no liners), with a high nitrogen content. Consequently, the pools are dark and the bottoms are not clearly visible. Bridges are mostly single planks with no handrails, which add a delightful sense of adventure when crossing the channels. Moorhens feed in the larger pools. The water level is higher than the Hoornsloot with simple timber dams, which are netted to exclude leaves and driftwood at times of high water levels.

There are five staff for a 5ha garden and the management is intensive. In fact, the gardeners and managers drive the design: for instance, the head gardener has a 'no hoe' policy. There is a small mess hut and enclosed storage area and notes about plants for the month are placed under an overhang of this hut. Naturally no chemicals (herbicides and pesticides) are used, and weeding and plant removal are done by hand. Pruning and thinning ensure light levels penetrate to the ground layer, always crucial in layered plantings. The effect is natural, but in fact this is a highly maintained and artificially gardened area.

A. The Thijssepark represents Dutch peat bog vegetation.
B. The gardeners are the heroines and heroes. Nearly all the garden maintenance is done by hand and of course no pesticides are used.
C. Tree growth is carefully controlled to allow light to reach the ground. The walks pass through a series of darker more enclosed areas which then open out into lighter areas.
D. One of the more open areas to the west of the *heempark*.
E. The water is black and the land is boggy. The channels are lightly dredged by hand annually with major dredging using machines every 30 years, most recently in 2012. Bridges are modest, narrow plank structures.

6
Education and Employment

Plant identification instruction at Hadlow College, Kent, UK

This chapter looks at the route to becoming a practising landscape architect, beginning with what you need to do while you are in preparatory education and then looking at different university courses and paths into full-time employment.

Applying for a university course

Landscape architecture is a discipline that straddles the sciences and arts. As such it is good to have studied art, geography and/or biology to a high level at school. Some schools may not offer art to final exam standard or to science students, in which case you should develop your drawing skills independently by taking evening classes or summer courses.

You can apply to study landscape architecture at university on leaving school but in many countries you can also apply after doing an undergraduate degree in something else. An earlier degree may range from the sciences to the arts, from geography and environmental sciences to fine art and fashion design.

When applying to university, use your portfolio to demonstrate your full range of artistic and design abilities. Some applicants make the mistake of thinking an admissions tutor is only looking for professional-standard planting plans or construction drawings. This is not the case. In fact, most are on the lookout for more general evidence of design potential, which might include school art projects, photography, clothes designed and made by the applicants, photographs of gardens they have created or worked in, flower arranging, graphic work, etc. As admissions tutors at Greenwich, we ask applicants to show us freehand line drawings of 3D forms

in 3D space – for example, a kitchen table with cups and saucers on it – because spatial design is crucial to landscape design. Note that admissions tutors are not necessarily expecting technical drawing competence, whether digital or manual, because that is normally taught on the university course. However, they will expect general computer literacy.

Applicants should be able to demonstrate their interest in landscape architecture by reference to their reading and visits made to landscape architecture and garden design projects. It's also a good idea to have done some work experience in a landscape architect's office. You should also attend public lectures and seminars given by professional landscape architecture associations. Remember: most admissions tutors are looking for evidence of an enquiring intelligence.

The nature of university courses varies from country to country but typically they will be:

- 50 per cent design-based, taught in a design studio;
- 25 per cent theoretical: the history of architecture and gardens, ecology, earth sciences;
- 25 per cent technical: technical drawing, digital design, horticulture, and construction.

Field trips and study tours enable students to understand the concepts of landscape architecture.

A. Field trip to temporary garden Union Street, London.
B. Visit to Grebbeberg overlooking the plain of the River Rhine in the Netherlands.
C. Paris field trip viewing the Parc Citroën-Cévennes.

Developing a portfolio of work examples is part
of professional life and starts with the putting
together of a range of skills for your interview.

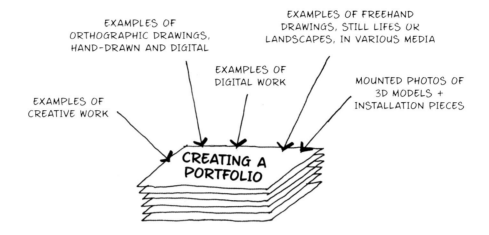

EXAMPLES OF
ORTHOGRAPHIC DRAWINGS,
HAND-DRAWN AND DIGITAL

EXAMPLES OF FREEHAND
DRAWINGS, STILL LIFES OR
LANDSCAPES, IN VARIOUS MEDIA

EXAMPLES OF
DIGITAL WORK

EXAMPLES OF
CREATIVE WORK

MOUNTED PHOTOS OF
3D MODELS +
INSTALLATION PIECES

CREATING A
PORTFOLIO

- UNDERSTAND WHY YOU NEED
  A PORTFOLIO

- WORK SHOULD BE SIMPLY
  MOUNTED AND TITLED

- ONLY INCLUDE WORK THAT
  YOU ARE PROUD OF

- ORGANIZE YOUR WORK IN
  A SEQUENCE YOU CAN
  TALK THROUGH

- AVOID PUTTING YOUR WORK
  IN PLASTIC SLEEVES

- SOME INSTITUTIONS HAVE

RIGOROUS PORTFOLIO
REQUIREMENTS FOR
APPLICANTS. SOME
REQUIRE DIGITAL
SUBMISSIONS.

A TYPICAL LANDSCAPE ARCHITECTURE PROGRAMME

Design programmes are usually 50 per cent design studio
taught, supported by technical and theoretical teaching.

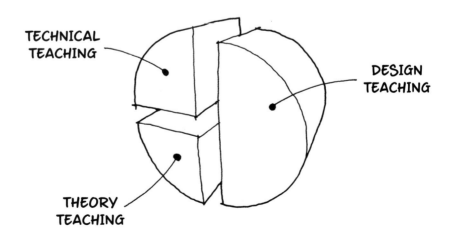

TECHNICAL
TEACHING

DESIGN
TEACHING

THEORY
TEACHING

Before landscape architecture was firmly established as a profession, individuals had to build up an educational framework themselves. For example, Bodfan Gruffydd in the 1930s began a gardening course at the Royal Horticultural Society at Wisley, Surrey, UK before going to New Zealand to work as secretary of the New Zealand Town Planning Institute. He then returned to Britain and completed a horticulture course at Bangor in Wales. He applied to become a member of the Institute of Landscape Architects during World War II and built up a private practice in landscape architecture, first in Wales and then in London. In the early 1950s he became landscape architect for Crawley New Town and in 1961 was involved in establishing the landscape architecture course at Cheltenham. Later he became president of the Institute of Landscape Architects and masterplanned Telford New Town. Such 'learning on the job', usually with a horticultural or architectural base, was typical of landscape architects in England in the 1940s and 1950s.

Nowadays there are specific courses in landscape architecture in many countries. These typically last five years, a model established at US Ivy League universities at the beginning of the twentieth century and consisting of a three-year Bachelor's degree followed by a two-year Master's. This is now the standard model in most countries.

The model is slightly different in the UK, where three-year Bachelor's degree courses are followed by a single-year professional Diploma or Master's. Four-year degree programmes are also to be found at the *Fachhochschulen*, also known as the *Hochschulen für Wirtschaft und Umwelt* (Universities of Applied Sciences), in Germany. One interesting variation is that of the *Akademie voor Bouwkunst* in Amsterdam, which offers a four-year part-time Master's degree (the staff work on it on a voluntary basis). There is also a more conventional two-year International Master's (or IMLA) run by the *Hochschule für Wirtschaft und Umwelt Nürtingen-Geislingen* (HfWU) in Baden-Württemberg and the *Hochschule Weihenstephan-Triesdorf* (HSWT) south of Munich in Bavaria.

As mentioned earlier, graduates can also change to landscape architecture by means of a two- or three-year Master's 'conversion' course, though this is more typical of the US and UK than elsewhere. In the US these conversion Master's are known as MLAs (Master's of Landscape Architecture). There are only a few such conversion courses in continental Europe, such as at the *Hochschule Anhalt* in Köthen in Saxony-Anhalt (with English and German language teaching). There is also a one-year Master's at the Zurich ETH, the Swiss Federal Institute of Technology, which is limited to graduates in architecture and landscape architecture. The University of Florence in Italy likewise offers a two-year conversion Master's to architecture graduates.

What course to choose? The best advice is to look at the work of graduates (as on websites and any annual exhibition), to visit the school, and to check university listings. Courses vary from those that are very scientifically based (many Polish and Russian courses are like this) to design-based schools often in art or architecture schools, to places where horticulture forms the basis. Russian schools emphasize forestry, of course, one of the Moscow schools is in the Forestry University.

It is also worth seeing whether any research is conducted at a school because this may benefit the teaching, for instance, in Europe, Wageningen, Sheffield and Zurich ETH are known for their research as are Harvard, MIT and Berkeley in the US. It is best to talk to current students when you visit. Guides to university education are available from many national associations of landscape architecture. Details of these national associations are listed on the website of the International Federation of Landscape Architects (IFLA): www.iflaonline.org/. There are also fairly comprehensive listings of European Schools on the website of the European Council of Landscape Architecture Schools (ECLAS) http://www.eclas.org/universities.php and there is a list of North American schools on the website of the American Society of Landscape Architects (ASLA) http://www.asla.org/schools.aspx covering the US and Canada (linked). The nearest to a worldwide listing of schools, though by no means complete, is on the Le Notre website (a European-based network of schools) http://www.le-notre.org/public/member-schools-universities.php

Otherwise go to each national association for advice.

Digital design is nowadays taught both formally and as an outcome to other design units.

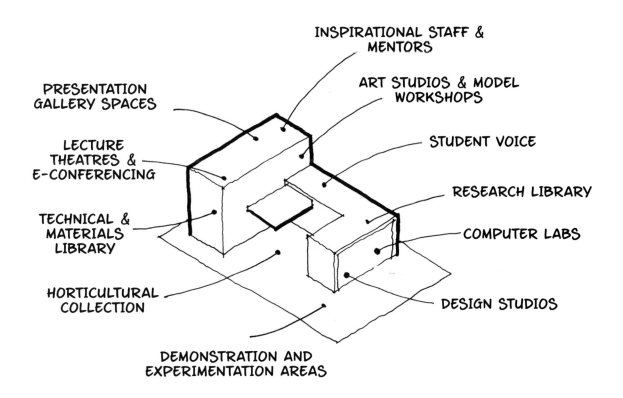

SKILLS YOU WILL NEED TO DEVELOP

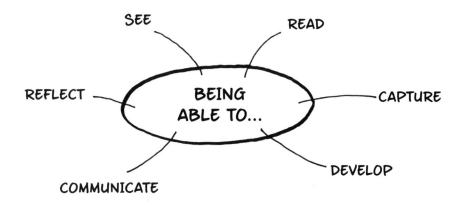

AFRICA:

Landscape architecture education in Africa is relatively undeveloped outside South Africa. Indeed, there are no landscape architecture schools in the whole of North Africa, including Egypt, that we know of (there are schools elsewhere in the Middle East such as in Lebanon, Israel, Palestine and Saudi Arabia). In South Africa there are currently three universities accredited by the state registration body, the South African Council for the Landscape Architectural Profession (SACLAP), and a further two awaiting accreditation. That at the University of Cape Town is a two-year conversion MLA. North of the Zambezi there appears to be the two established courses at Jomo Kenyatta University of Agriculture and Technology in Nairobi and a Master of Landscape Architecture (M.Land.Arch.) at Uganda Martyrs University in Kampala which follows a Bachelor of Environmental Design. There are national associations in Kenya (a chapter of the Association of Architects), Morocco, Malawi and Nigeria as well as in South Africa.

ASIA:

In Asia many of the national associations list schools. The biggest increase in the past two decades has been in China, where there are now large numbers of landscape architecture schools: contact the Chinese Society of Landscape Architects for further details (www.chsla. org.cn/english.htm). There are separate associations in Taiwan (www.clasit.org. tw/) and Hong Kong (http://www.hkila. com/v2/) where there is a conversion MLA at the University of Hong Kong. In the People's Republic, the English-language site to start searching for landscape architecture schools is the website of the Chinese College and Admissions System (CUCAS), www.cucas. edu.cn/, which is aimed at international students, as well as approaching the Chinese Society of Landscape Architects for further details. CUCAS lists about 70 landscape architecture programmes, but this is only selective. By contrast, the Indian Society of Landscape Architects (established in 2003) lists only four schools (www.isola.org.in/site/about). In South-East Asia there is landscape architecture education in Thailand, Korea, Malaysia, Indonesia and the Philippines. Further west, in Iran and in the Middle

East, there are now a number of schools, including the well-established American University of Beirut, a number in Saudi Arabia and one at Birzeit University in Ramallah, Palestine. The Israel Institute of Technology is in Haifa.

Generally first approach the national association for up-to-date advice.

AUSTRALASIA:

There are comprehensive listings of schools in Australia and New Zealand, where the profession has been well established since at least the 1970s. The Australian Institute of Landscape Architects (www.aila.org.au/) has accredited eight university programmes; the New Zealand Institute of Landscape Architects equivalent has accredited three (www.nzila.co.nz/become-a-landscape-architect/how-can-i-become-a-la.aspx).

CENTRAL AND SOUTH AMERICA:

Brazil is the biggest country in South America. Unfortunately the national professional body, the Associação Brasileira de Arquitetos Paisagistas (ABAP), http://www.abap.org.br/index.htm does not currently appear to list them, but courses in landscape architecture exist at the University of São Paulo. In Argentina there are four undergraduate programmes and eight postgraduate programmes listed on the website of the Argentine professional body, the Centro Argentino de Arquitectos Paisajistas (CAAP), http://www.caapaisajistas.org. ar/ . In Chile the Instituto Chileno de Arquitectos del Paisaje (ICHAP) http:// www.ichap.cl/links.php lists seven schools. While the Sociedad Colombiana de Arquitectos Paisajistas (SAP) in Colombia lists seven undergraduate level and one Master's programme.

EUROPE:

IFLA Europe operates a school recognition system in conjunction with the national associations and has a country-by-country listing including a total of 50 schools – for instance, seven of the nineteen German schools and four of the fifteen Landscape Institute-accredited schools in the UK. The IFLA Europe recognition is not comprehensive because applications are on a voluntary basis. There is as yet no totally comprehensive pan-European listing, so students are advised to approach

their national association. However, the website of the European Council of Landscape Architecture Schools (ECLAS) lists the majority of landscape architecture programmes and schools in Western Europe (www.eclas.org/study-programmes-courses.php), although its coverage of Russia and the former Soviet bloc countries (the CIS states) is not complete. The ECLAS listing also includes research institutes, so do check with the individual school as not every school mentioned offers undergraduate education. A more comprehensive survey conducted by one of the authors for IFLA Europe in 2008 listed 125 schools across the continent.

NORTH AMERICA:

The American Society of Landscape Architects (ASLA) website's education area (http://www.asla.org/schools.aspx) lists landscape architecture schools in the US. Most states have at least one. Schools are accredited by the professional association, ASLA, via the Landscape Architectural Accreditation Board (LAAB), a body run by the US professional association which also vets the five schools accredited in Canada by the Canadian Society of Landscape Architects, including that at the Université de Montréal which is, of course, French-speaking. Note licensure (registration) is a separate state-based system. The Council of Educators in Landscape Architecture (CELA) also publishes a list of schools which covers the North American schools as well as a few in other continents http://www.thecela. org/school-list.php?alpha=u.

A

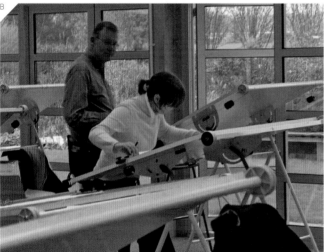

B

C

Different institutions have diverse studio spaces; many are multi-use transitional spaces rather than dedicated studios.

A. Charette studio at Lille School of Architecture and Landscape: working all day and all night in groups in a one-week urban planning study with students from Lille and Greenwich.
B. Technical drawing class using drawing boards.
C. First-year design studio, Istanbul Technical University

Developing a passion for plants and horticulture starts with guided plant identifications and nursery visits, and is reinforced with field trips to construction sites and specialist gardens.

A. Students inspecting the Hilliers Tree Nursery that supplied the large stock of clipped hedge plants for the London 2012 Olympic Park.

B. Plant 'idents' introduce students to both Latin nomenclature and physical forms of the plant, and are backed up by regular plant identification exams.

C. Inspecting semi-mature tree stock, and discussing how to select trees.

D. Horticulturist lecturers give students a clear insight to design and management issues.

Internships and jobs

In North America, government agencies such as the US National Park Service operate a well-established programme of internships. This system is also emulated by some private practitioners: SWA and EDSA internships (both landscape architecture firms) have a good reputation, for instance. Structured systems providing internships are less common elsewhere, though the Dutch State Forestry Service, the *Staatsbosbeheer*, offers them in its landscape architecture section. Otherwise work experience is more usually gained by individuals approaching particular practices directly. A general international internship guide is published on the IFLA Europe website (http://europe.iflaonline.org/?ck=2012-6-5-15-49-2).

JOBS

Potential employers prefer to receive a postal application. Whether you're applying for a job or an unpaid, short-term internship, send a covering letter, a short, two-page curriculum vitae and some drawing work (say, six or seven examples) on A4 paper. Send CDs only as back-up. Note: do not email material in the first place: landscape architects are busy people and it takes time to download attachments. Indeed, many email hosts block large attachments from unknown senders. Address letters personally to a named individual in a practice, preferably a principal; if going for an interview, research the practice beforehand. Do not expect an acknowledgement for applications – though it is always nice to receive one.

The university year in many countries runs from September to June. So a good time to apply for a job is in September or October (August tends to be quiet) or at the beginning of the year, from January until April, when graduating students will not be applying. If you are about to graduate it can be a good tactic to take a summer-long internship, then look for a permanent post as a graduate of landscape architecture in the autumn.

Different practices specialize in different forms of work, from a garden-scale to environmental assessment and environmental consultancy. Often it is good to aim to follow a project from the beginning through to the end so you can see the full range of work from inception to work on site.

THE POSITION OF THE INTERN WITHIN A PRACTICE STRUCTURE

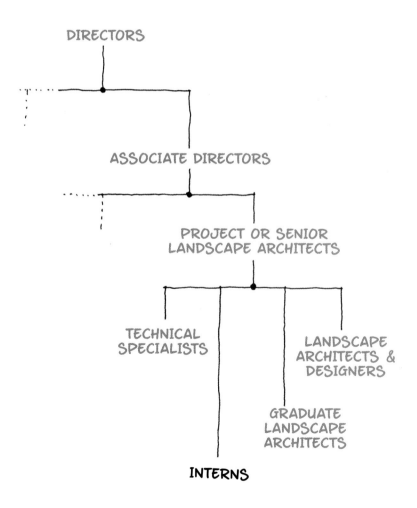

Setting up your own business

Not everyone wants to work for someone else. In particular, graduate conversion students are making a career change and may wish to establish their own practice. And landscape architecture is particularly suitable for starter businesses because many practices are just one or two people.

How do you get started? Strategic planning is fundamental to any marketing effort and to branding and positioning a practice. To do this, you need to have a clear view of the market and also what you can offer. For example, at the time of writing, new housing construction is depressed in the UK, but there is a market for projects related to the estates of the very rich, Russian and Middle Eastern plutocrats, particularly if one has a special reputation for work on historic gardens, conservation, planting design or sustainable development. Recessions are good times to set up your own practice supported perhaps by freelance or teaching work, while working on public design competitions to establish a reputation. And as the population grows, there will be inevitably an increase in the new housing building market when the economy recovers from the post-2008 downturn. In the US the Bureau of Labor Statistics forecasts that the already mature profession of land architecture will need to grow by 16 per cent in the decade 2010–20 (www.bls. gov/ooh/Architecture-and-Engineering/ Landscape-architects.htm). Market research is thus vital to the survival and growth of your practice. Have a clear idea of what markets exist and what markets might be opening up in the future. Areas in the UK where investment is planned for the future include high-speed railways and, in Scotland and Wales, the reopening of closed railways – environmental impact assessment is critical in such projects. It might therefore make sense to establish a market niche in visual assessment or noise limitation so that you can find work as a subconsultant to bigger firms.

The economies of China, India and Brazil are still growing. Part of the challenge in these economies is to convince the market that landscape architecture and the related advice the profession can offer on sustainability issues and the like are important for developers, whether in the private or state sector. In China the other challenge is to ensure consultancy services are valued for themselves.

'START-UP' COMPACT OFFICE

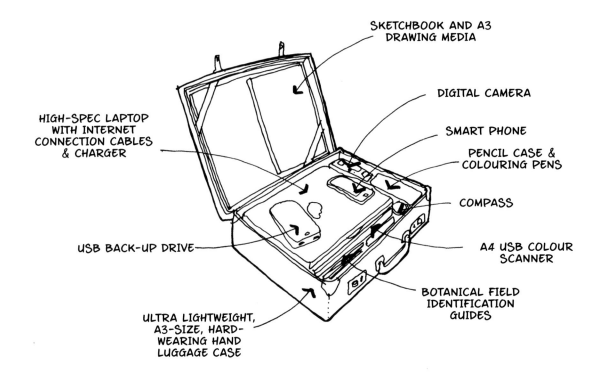

SKETCHBOOK AND A3 DRAWING MEDIA

DIGITAL CAMERA

SMART PHONE

PENCIL CASE & COLOURING PENS

COMPASS

A4 USB COLOUR SCANNER

BOTANICAL FIELD IDENTIFICATION GUIDES

HIGH-SPEC LAPTOP WITH INTERNET CONNECTION CABLES & CHARGER

USB BACK-UP DRIVE

ULTRA LIGHTWEIGHT, A3-SIZE, HARD-WEARING HAND LUGGAGE CASE

Marketing

Until the late twentieth century, active marketing was not considered appropriate for any profession in most countries. Commissions were obtained by making submissions in competitions, being listed on professional registers, networking, such as joining local business organizations, chambers of commerce and charities, and via the telephone directory. This situation changed in the 1980s in response to fresh free-market thinking and a general wish to promote competition. Now all professions can advertise in many countries, and competitive consultancy fee tendering is the rule – though the downside of this is that often the cheapest wins. Cheapest is not necessarily best or most appropriate. Marketing accounts for a significant proportion of landscape architects' annual expenditure. Such

marketing will probably be much more than a brochure or a website – it requires a brand identity, a way of projecting what is particular about a private practice: the values, ideas, design knowledge, experience and philosophy that distinguishes a practice. High-quality branding, though, will not compensate for an inability to work to schedule and budget or to get along with clients. If you agree a budget and a timescale, then work to it. But before doing that, ensure first that the budget is adequate and the timescale workable.

Networking is as important as it has always been. Informal contact with potential clients should be pursued, so attend conferences organized by bodies serving potential clients such as government agencies, developers,

railway and transport organizations, museums, historic buildings, the education sector, etc.

Giving a paper at a conference or trade show is often a more effective way of advertising your skills than paying for a stand. Similarly, editorial articles are a preferable form of publicity to adverts or appearances in listings, since they allow you – whether as the writer or subject of a piece – to explain what you do in detail.

It is good practice for the principals of a practice to spend some time annually in a retreat or away from the office with an outside mentor to review progress and plans for the future.

Olin is a medium-sized landscape architecture practice based in Philadelphia and Los Angeles, with 87 staff. Set up by Professor Laurie Olin they have overseen projects such as Bryant Park, New York, and the Washington Monument landscape Washington, D.C. They appointed their first Director of Technology, Chris Hanley, in 2005. Now they have their own practice-based wiki, called KnowledgeBase, which might be opened to subscription. Olin holds regular in-house tutorial new design tool sessions, and because often the software is based on architectural practice (because it is the industry standard) they change the software to suit landscape architecture. 'We're not going to let the tool dictate our design,' says Chris Hanley. The Olin crew takes on developer languages like Python and Rhinoscript and adapts the design software. Laurie Olin also sits on the the board of the Gehry Technologies US building industry-wide initiative, set up in late 2011, aiming to develop further BIM (Building Information Modelling) and Integrated Project Delivery, which so aims to 'transform the building industry and the practice of design'.

Thames Landscape Strategy

Cultural landscapes and a long-term vision

Kim Wilkie studied modern history at Oxford and then environmental design at the University of California, Berkeley, before returning to England to set up his own landscape practice in 1989. An interest in cultural landscapes led him to put together 'a 100-year blueprint' for the Thames, a proposal to provide public access along the River Thames from Hampton to Kew that would give added value to the river's landscape as a cultural entity, a distinct area with historic and aesthetic value. This he describes as an 'Arcadian landscape... of palaces, villas, and parks' interspersed with 'workmanlike sections of boat yards'.

The choice of the Thames between Hampton and Kew was based on its role as what Wilkie calls 'the cradle of the English Landscape Movement', particularly in the views from Richmond Hill (see opposite). There is also a range of significant sites along this part of the river: the botanic gardens at Kew, the expansive Richmond and Bushey Parks, the palaces of Richmond and Hampton Court, along with historic buildings at Syon Park, Marble Hill Park, Ham House and other important buildings such as Garrick's Villa at Hampton and Pope's Strawberry Hill.

The proposal was first presented as an exhibition, *Thames Connections*, for the Royal Fine Art Commission in 1991. This led to a commission by another central government agency, the Countryside Commission (now Natural England), which in turn gave rise to the Thames Landscape Strategy, developed in 1991–94 and covering nearly 20km of riverside from Hampton to Kew, and focusing particularly on historic views, avenues and vistas. Published in 1994 it was adopted by the Secretary of State for the Environment, the central government minister, as a framework for planning policies along the Thames. Indeed it has been extended eastwards through London to the mouth of the River Thames. It is described as a '100-year vision' (which is also really a landscape architect's minimum timeframe). It also works with the Thames Waterways Plan and the Mayor's Blue Ribbon Network. The work has continued over three decades and the Thames Landscape Strategy is a 'live planning forum' supported by five local councils, and at a national level.

Wilkie describes the Thames as an 'extraordinary landscape' and he began to plot views. Sometimes the work is very simple, very soft and gentle such as bringing willow edges to the margins and fighting Japanese knotweed, sometimes interventions such as mile-long avenues, sometimes stopping planning permission for new buildings, sometimes encouraging new development and realizing the 'rhythm of built and unbuilt'. This is also about 'taking the environment rather seriously as a flood alleviation corridor'.

It has also led to further projects in the twenty-first century, including the Pastoral Arcadia aimed at conserving, interpreting and restoring the views from Richmond Hill and Floodscape in Richmond, which is working to restore the ancient flood meadows by the Thames. As Kim Wilkie advises, 'the accessibility of the study and the support and continued involvement of the local community means that the landscape character for once is the basis for planning decisions and funding investment'.

A. Bird's-eye analysis of the landscape character on the Isleworth stretch of the river, with vistas (in red) from the King's Observatory and along the river.
B. Pastoral Arcadia aims to conserve and enhance the views from Richmond Hill.
C. The pattern of the landscape along and centred on the Thames, so often an administrative divide, Kim Wilkie's study sees it as cultural whole, as he says 'Only by trying to understand how these elements interact with the memory or myths of past settlement, can one begin to tease out Pope's *genius loci* – the spirit of the place.'
D&E. Before-and-after view of walks across Richmond Hill. Sometimes the changes are small: simplifying, rustifying and removing municipal clutter.

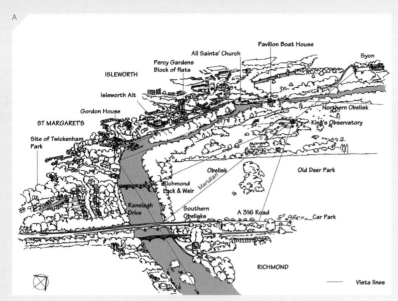

A

B

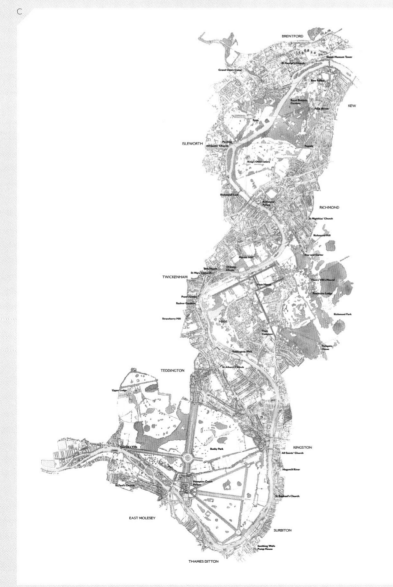

C

D

E

A note on professional status: the way the profession is seen worldwide

There are two models for establishment of the profession found internationally: state registration or licensure (US usage) and no state registration, no protection of title, but recognized and accepted by government and other professions. Title protection restricts the right to use the term 'Landscape Architect' to state-registered landscape architects.

In the US, state licensure is found in 49 states of the Union, and is required in order to be able to practise in those states. There are two forms of state licensure: in the majority of the states the act is a Practice Act which prohibits unlicensed people from calling themselves landscape architects or from practising the profession. In a minority – the exceptions are Massachusetts, Maine and Illinois – there is a Title Act whereby unlicensed individuals may not use the title of landscape architect but may still do the work. The Practice Act is the stronger protecton. Licensure requires education and also work experience and the passing of the Landscape Architect Registration Examination (L.A.R.E.), based on the Council of Landscape Architectural Registration Board's guidelines.

In several European countries (Germany, the Netherlands, Austria, Hungary, Czech Republic, Slovakia and nominally in Italy) there is also state registration. In most, there is a national register based purely on education. In Germany the system is based at the *Länder* (federal state) level via registration with the *Architektenkammer* or chamber of architects. In Hungary there is also a work experience requirement. The 'nominal' status in Italy is because of an invidious position in that a Master's degree is required to become a member of the *Consiglio Nazionale degli Architetti, Pianificatori, Paesaggisti e Conservatori* (CNAPPC) and yet a full undergraduate course leading to Master's-level education in landscape architecture was only introduced in the 1990s. In consequence many members of the national association of landscape architects, the *Associazione Italiana di Architettura del Paesaggio* (AIAPP), cannot register with the national *Consiglio* – however, graduates of Master's programmes in architecture can.

Elsewhere, in Hong Kong there is a Landscape Architects Registration Board, set up by the Hong Kong Landscape Architects Registration Ordinance of 1997 for the Special Administrative Zone of Hong Kong (http://www.larb.com.hk/First_Page.htm) and in South Africa professional membership is with the South African Council for the Landscape Architectural Profession (www.saclap.org.za).

The other model may be termed the Scandinavian or North-west European one, where there is no state register but the profession is well established. There are landscape architects represented in government commissions and on advisory boards. This is the position in Scandinavia, the UK, some countries in Central Europe and Australia and New Zealand. Some would argue that in the UK the Royal Charter protects the title 'Chartered Landscape Architect', but this is a technicality, and you don't have to be a member of the Landscape Institute to practise as a landscape architect and call yourself a landscape architect: in the UK there is no protection of the title 'landscape architect'.

In a few countries the title 'landscape architect' cannot be used at all because of legislation protecting the status of architects and therefore the use of that word. As a result, landscape architects in Spain may not call themselves *arquitecto paesajista* (though the term is commonly used in South America); instead they call themselves *paesajistas*. In France there is a parallel situation: landscape architects call themselves *paysagistes* and are not allowed to use the title *architecte paysagiste* as their colleagues in Francophone Canada, Switzerland and Belgium do. However, in France the profession of *paysagiste* is otherwise well established.

A. The profession at international level,
   EFLA 2008 General Assembly, Brussels.
B. IFLA General Assembly, Apeldoorn, the
   Netherlands, 2008.
C. ECLAS conference, Genoa, Italy, 2009.

Druk White Lotus School, Ladakh, India

Sustainable building in a hostile environment

Druk White Lotus School (DWLS) is a school for 750 pupils from nursery age to 18. The school is surrounded by mountains of the Zanskar and Ladakh ranges, rising to over 6,000m high in the Himalaya range. First planned in 1997, it was designed by Arup Associates with staff seconded on an unpaid basis and is supported by the Drukpa Trust, a UK-registered charity.

Two monasteries, Shey and Thikse, overlook the school site and it lies near the River Indus, with its lush vegetation. Ladakh is on a similar latitude to Egypt and is classified as a cold desert. Where irrigation water is available, growing conditions are excellent for half the year. Everything is then frozen for the other half of the year with temperatures falling to -30°C.

The first phase, the nursery and infant school, opened in September 2001 with a junior school in 2005. The buildings then suffered severe damage from a mudslide in 2010. The site had been chosen without landscape advice and much of the site was buried in mud to a depth of one metre. The area is also in an earthquake zone. This dramatizes the need for a sustainable landscape plan and has led to the involvement of landscape architecture staff and students from a number of British universities.

Ladakh is regarded as the 'canary in the coal mine' for global warming. The glaciers are retreating and the volume of meltwater is decreasing. In response, the school is a model of sustainable development, water supply is from boreholes supplied by solar-powered pumps and the building materials are local. Traditional dry latrines are improved and fly-free. The building is constructed of willow timber frame (from local monastic plantations), the inner walls are of mud bricks and the outer cladding is of local granite. Water is pumped from 30m below ground level to a 16,000-gallon tank at the top of the site to supply the school with water and to irrigate the gardens.

Buddhism remains a strong influence in the region and the DWLS was initiated by His Holiness the Gyalwang Drukpa. His wish is to conserve Buddhist traditions while also learning from the modern world. This is reflected in the landscape design. Arup's layout for the school buildings was based on a mandala. The school landscape design draws on other Buddhist symbols and on the landscape types that characterize Ladakh: they include meadows, orchards, vegetable gardens, small woodlands and native habitats of various kinds.

Work on the landscape plan began on site in 2012 with the involvement of Sheffield and Greenwich universities. Typical is the work of landscape architecture student Simon Brown from Greenwich, who has helped set up an on-site plant nursery and worked with the local construction team under the construction manager Sonam Angdus and his Nepali labourers, and with Madov Shresth, the head gardener, on clearing mudslide damage inside the new mudslide wall, the construction of new earthworks, installing irrigation, sorting out and manuring the soil and planting through the summer of 2012. He has also helped on workshops with the schoolchildren.

A. The granite-clad classroooms of the school, beyond are the white walls and golden roofs of the Naro Phodrang (Naropa Palace) and the mountain setting. The site is to the east of the fertile flood plain of the River Indus.
B. In summer temperatures are relatively mild and the outdoor spaces can become gardens for teaching.
C. Construction work in 2012, after all traces of the 2010 mudslide had been removed.

7
The Future

The Iberian peninsula at night, 4 December 2011, NASA astronaut photograph, with Portugal in the foreground, Spain in the middle centred on Madrid, Africa to the right, and France top and left (with the Bay of Biscay in black) with its lights subdued by cloud. The image opposite shows energy emissions in the form of light, across a sizeable portion of south-west Europe. Could these lights indicate a species, *homo sapiens*, which is overreaching its dominance?

'A sense of crisis has brought us together. What is merely offensive or disturbing today threatens life itself tomorrow. We are concerned over misuse of the environment and development which has lost all contact with the basic processes of nature. Lake Erie is becoming septic, New York City is short of water, the Delaware River is infused with salt, the Potomac River with sewage and silt. Air is polluted in major cities and their citizens breathe and see with difficulty. Most urban Americans are being separated from visual and physical contact with nature in any form. All too soon life in such polluted environments will be the national human experience.'

Declaration of founding members of the US Landscape Architecture Foundation, June 1966, at Independence Hall in Philadelphia, US, Campbell Miller, Grady Clay, Ian L. McHarg, Charles R. Hammond, George E. Patton, John O. Simonds

A changing environment

As this book is being written, nearly 50 years after the Philadelphia Declaration above, the world economy is passing through what might euphemistically be called 'interesting times'. There is expansion in Asia and South America and growth in China, India, Indonesia, Brazil and Australasia. With demand for raw resources fed by growth rates of up to 10 per cent, there is a worldwide rise in commodity prices and Africa is increasingly seen not only as a source of such materials but also as providing fresh land for agricultural production. Meanwhile much of the Western world – Europe and North America, but also Japan – is experiencing little or no economic growth, and the future of the Eurozone is being questioned.

In the greater scheme of history, the Western world's relative economic downturn can be viewed as a passing phase in the mid term (though hopefully one that will lead to more effective regulation of the banking industry) and clearly there is a rebalancing of the economies between East and West and North and South. Western economic dominance is recent – only 300–400 years at most – for most of the past 2,000 years the leading centres of sophisticated technology and cultural development were centred on China and India.

However, the long-term trends are for a threefold increase in world population, in demand for raw materials and in urban populations as a proportion of total population. In consequence Planet Earth is under pressure from a variety of factors, including:

- loss of biodiversity;
- net increase in the human ecological footprint;
- climate change and in consequence fluctuations in extreme weather conditions as well as sea level rise and flooding, and a threat to the water supply;
- shortage of raw materials.

Landscape architects have a contribution to make in tackling all of these issues.

Let us recapitulate briefly the development of landscape architecture. Its precursor, landscape gardening, was a visual and scenic profession, primarily serving a private market of kings and landed gentry. Landscape architecture thus began in the nineteenth century as a visual profession, based on an inheritance from garden and park design but now reorientated to serve communities in the new industrial towns and to realize ideas of wilderness protection and agricultural development for society as a whole.

In the twentieth century this mission was overlain with an interest in nature conservation and ecology. In the twenty-first century anxieties about ecological health have given rise to a concern for the whole landscape, and to a focus on sustainability. In the future landscape architects' primary task promises to be related to finding ways of sustainable living for a predominantly urbanized world (human) population.

LANDSCAPE MISSION

The focus of landscape architecture has evolved over the last two centuries, gradually widening its influence over the design process.

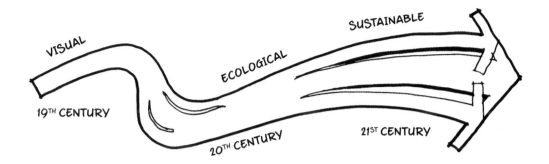

New sustainable technologies have an increasing impact on the environment.

A. Demonstration installation of a planted biofiltration wall.
B. Wind turbines line a Dutch motorway.
C. Solar panels providing power for isolated restaurant on Ilha Deserta in the Parque Natural da Ria Formosa, Faro, Portugal.

A

B

A. View across Sangam Nagar slum towards Antop Hill in Mumbai.
B. A home to 200,000+ people and one of the largest slums in Mumbai with an estimated population density of 3000/ha.
C. Downtown New Orleans after floods caused by Hurricane Katrina in 2005: 53 levee breaches, 80 per cent of the city flooded, over 700 people dead and about $81 billion of property damage.

Some challenges

WATER

Water is a key resource. Already desalination plants dot the Mediterranean littoral, while in London, Thames Water opened the £250 million Beckton desalination plant in 2010: south-east England is a water deficit area in most summers. A restructuring of infrastructure is following: national trunk water networks, solar power farms, wind farms, retro-fitting of existing buildings with insulation and solar power, wind farms, and nuclear fission (or maybe nuclear fusion in the light of the Three Mile Island, Chernobyl and Fukishima disasters), biomass as a fuel for power stations (and development of ethanol fuels) and densification of development to minimize energy use. Denmark has achieved figures of 25 per cent of energy from sustainable sources.

Urbanization increases river flow and storms overwhelm a river basin, hence the Rhine floods of 1995 and 2007. For example, the watershed of the Rhine has lost 80 per cent of its flood plains and the Elbe 85 per cent in the past century: and increasingly a permeable landscape has been overlain by an impermeable townscape. European cities have expanded in area by 79 per cent since the 1950s.

WATER SUPPLY AND FLOODING

In China (as elsewhere) growth is threatened by limits to the water supply. Water is fed by the glaciers in the Himalayas: the result of their retreat will be both flooding and drought. Flooding is a consequence of winter snows no longer being held in the mountains as glacier ice but instead draining quickly into China's rivers. Drought will be the consequence of reduction in the waterflow of rivers in summer as the glacier supply of summer meltwater reduces. Drought is not only a consequence of climate warming but also due to the extraction of river water by industry and agriculture and the consequent diminution of downstream supplies. The north is short of water whereas the south has a greater supply. One response has been the South–North Water Transfer Project, which aims to move water from the Yangtze River to the Yellow River and the Hai River.

Everywhere industry, farming and the growing population are competing for a finite supply of water. As a result, groundwater levels are falling as artesian water (that held in aquifers) is drained, and the remaining supplies are threatened by contamination from agriculture and industry. The nitrification of groundwater due to run-off of agricultural fertilizer is increasing across the world.

One response is to create a national water policy like that in the Netherlands, which relates and connects water supply with both river flooding and sea level rises.

C

The Dutch National Water Plan

A national flood and water quality policy

The Dutch National Water Plan was adopted in 2009, following nearly ten years of consultation and discussion. It focuses on prevention and management of sea and river-related flooding.

In 2000 the Dutch adopted a new approach to flooding. Rather than a policy aiming at total prevention, they switched to a policy of accommodation, giving rivers space to flood. River water is diverted into auxiliary channels and wetlands or river marshland. This is less expensive and minimizes the adverse effects of flooding.

The Dutch State National Water Plan also aims to ensure access to clean water. In part this requires local action such as fertilizer and pollution controls, but also at a transnational level as its rivers also run through Germany, Belgium and France. The European Union European Water Framework Directive of 2000 aimed to address river and water pollution issues. Coastal flood defences are also being strengthened against sea flooding by measures that include adding to offshore sand sea defences with sand replenishment. Some 12 million m³ of sand are being placed annually on the beaches off the coastline to strengthen current sea defences.

Of course, these policies are national in scope and many professions contributed to the discussion that finally led to their formulation: Dutch landscape architects, for instance, developed scenarios for both river flooding and sea defences. The most dramatic was the West 8 proposal for a new series of islands, the Happy Isles, off the Dutch and Belgian coasts as an extension of the policy of offshore sandfill; the largest, Hollandsoog, was to be over 150,000ha in size. Both Dirk Sijmons, the first Dutch state landscape advisor, appointed in 2004, and Yttje Feddes, his successor in 2008, have been heavily involved in these proposals.

In 2005, the Dutch used their experience to advise the US on the river-flooding challenges in New Orleans, highlighted by Hurricane Katrina.

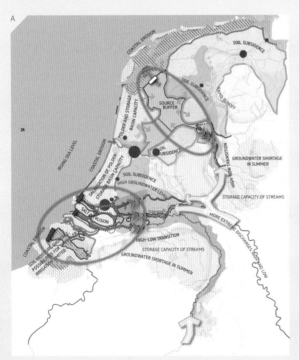

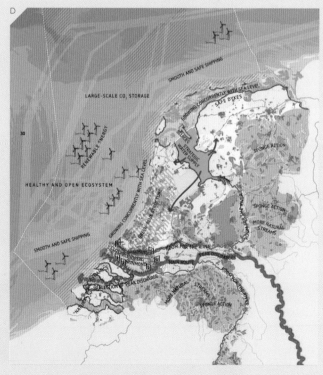

A. Key Water Tasks vary from control of salination
    along the North Sea coastline, soil subsidence
    in the north to summer groundwater shortage
    in the east.
B. National Flood Risk Map: the blues are areas of
    maximum water depth, with the darkest blue
    greater than 5m.
C. Ijsselmeer area: the largest freshwater lakes
    in NW Europe, used for water supply.
D. Target Situation: protection from sea level rise
    is by the dune system shown in yellow, the red
    lines show the dyke system; the blue of the
    Ijsselmeer forms the strategic water reserve;
    to the east are areas that would be used as a
    'sponge' effect and more natural streams; the
    seas would provide renewable energy (wind
    farms), shipping lanes and sub-seabed CO_2
    storage in depleted gas fields.

LOSS OF FORESTS

The UN Food and Agricultural Organization (FAO) reports that primary forests are being lost or modified at the rate of 6 million ha per annum. There has been widespread loss of forest cover in Indonesia, Africa and South America. This process contributes to global warming, sometimes dramatically, for example, in the forest fires of recent years in South-East Asia such as in Indonesia in 1997–98 or the 2005 Malaysian Haze. Such forest fires caused by slash-and-burn forest-clearance techniques also affect air quality and health, not to mention causing a major loss of natural habitat and, in consequence, of biodiversity.

Vegetation is necessary for the production of oxygen. *Homo sapiens* is dependent on oxygen, an element that reacts very readily, combining with other elements to form compounds: for instance, with iron to make rust (ferrous oxide). It is therefore a fugitive gas and easily disappears. Some 2.8 billion years ago, in what is known as the Great Oxidation Event, the levels of oxygen in the earth's atmosphere rose sufficiently to be able to support life as we know it. Oxygen was and is produced by cyanobacteria, or blue-green algae. These microbes perform photosynthesis using energy from sunshine, water and carbon dioxide to produce carbohydrates and oxygen. All plants need symbiotic cyanobacteria (chloroplasts) to do their photosynthesis. Without plants and photosynthesis atmospheric oxygen levels will fall. Without oxygen we die.

What does this mean for landscape architecture? First, it should influence specification of materials, including timber, ensuring that they come from sustainable sources, so primary forest is not felled; second, it should influence the nature of any development in tropical forest areas. In both North America and Europe, landscape architects advise on forestry development; in Russia, landscape architects graduate in forestry schools and are known as green engineers; in China, where landscape architects are also taught in forestry schools, major efforts have been made to increase forestry. This expertise can be used to protect surviving virgin or primary forest and to extend forestry planting in the form of secondary forests, particularly in the Tropics. At a masterplan scale always plant trees, and in towns plant street trees.

POPULATION GROWTH AND URBANIZATION

The global population is likely to grow from 6.9 billion in 2010 to 8.8 billion by 2040, according to UN figures, with many enjoying increasing prosperity accompanied by burgeoning material expectations. Ninety per cent of the planet's people live on 10 per cent of the land, and about 90 per cent of people live north of the equator. Dealing with this ever-increasing urban population requires densification to minimize loss of finite resources and a move to a low-carbon economy to reduce global warming. Land management and planning are key in achieving both of these.

The European Protection Agency has identified urban sprawl as a major problem. Elsewhere, the movement of people from the countryside to towns has led to the creation of megacities, cities or conurbations with populations of more than ten million. There are currently over 26 of them, including Tokyo (34 million people), Guangzhou (25 million) and New York (22 million).

Randstad – the Rotterdam, Den Haag, Amsterdam and Utrecht conurbation which forms a linear city around Green Heart Holland– offers an interesting contrast to many of these conurbations. Although its population is only 7,100,000, it offers a model for an extended multi-centred settlement which enables citizens to cycle out into the countryside in under half an hour.

A. Living walls help to remediate air quality, temperature and provide acoustic baffling: La Défense, Paris.
B. Sustainable drainage for water conservation, Dresden: re-using site construction materials.
C. Plane street trees in Alma Grove, the result of street beautification policies of the 1920s in Bermondsey, London.

THE VALUE OF TREES

Phytoremediation means the improvement of an environment due to plant growth. The term is used particularly in reference to the mitigation of metal, pesticide and oil pollution in soil and water. Specific plants achieve this by accumulating toxins in their own cells, or by degrading them or otherwise rendering them harmless.

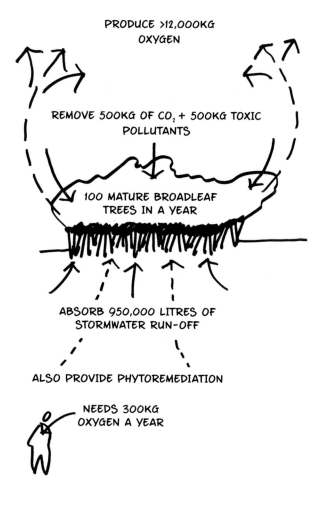

PRODUCE >12,000KG OXYGEN

REMOVE 500KG OF CO_2 + 500KG TOXIC POLLUTANTS

100 MATURE BROADLEAF TREES IN A YEAR

ABSORB 950,000 LITRES OF STORMWATER RUN-OFF

ALSO PROVIDE PHYTOREMEDIATION

NEEDS 300KG OXYGEN A YEAR

Floating Gardens, Shad Thames, London

Greening affordable housing in the city centre

Since 1999, Floating Gardens have grown up on more than thirty houseboats linked by walkways and bridges just a stone's throw from Tower Bridge in central London. Originally set up by architect Nicholas Lacey in the 1980s the houseboats have occupied the historic Downing Roads commercial moorings just downstream of the bridge. The gardens were created by residents initially led by Elaine Hughes, a former Greenwich landscape architecture graduate.

About 70 people live in the Downings Road moorings, at the foot of luxurious and expensive loft-style apartments in a floating community. The moorings have existed since the first half of the nineteenth century and are one of the Thames's oldest in continuous use.

The plants grow in 40cm-deep metal planters with a growing medium of 50 per cent topsoil and 50 per cent compost. Nearly all kitchen waste is composted in bins on the barges. The drainage on the barges is so good that they need a daily soaking in summer. The dry soil means that trees, including *Robinia pseudoacacia*, false acacias, do not reach their full potential. During droughts, water is pumped straight from the Thames, yet the salty tidal water has no obvious detrimental effects.

The plants include seaside and roof-garden planting which tolerate the desiccating winds on the Thames: waxy, silver-leafed and evergreen plants such as *Stipa tenuissima* and lavender and *Euphorbia amygdaloides robbiae* and ferns complemented by apple trees and low box.

The gardens attract waterfowl. But despite the introduction of stacks of rotting logs to attract bugs, this remains something of an unbalanced ecosystem, because of its isolated island nature.

Many of the boats on the moorings are historically significant, and they include barges, lighters, commercial tugs, Humber Keels, freight carriers, and both sail and motor barges from all over Europe.

The community practises 'time banking', a concept developed by the New Economics Foundation thinktank, which seeks to 'inspire and demonstrate real economic well-being'. People can earn and spend time credits. For instance, if a neighbour gives you an hour of her time – say, teaching you to knit – she earns a credit which she can 'spend' on someone else's time. In other words, the residents help each other out. It helps them get to know each other and establish a culture of trust.

A. Garden barge *Scrip*: seven of Nicholas Lacey's barges are garden barges.
B. Affordable housing in the centre of London.
C. The boats include Thames barges, Thames lighters, old commercial tugs, Humber keels, European river barges, and both sail and motor barges.
D. Top left, the communal stage, here used for dining.
E-G. A cheap and pleasant place to live in the centre of the city, a barge can cost from £100,000 and mooring costs can be £5–6,000 annually.

BIODIVERSITY LOSS

The growth of urban areas, the increasing rate of consumption of resources and anthropogenic (human-made) climate change are combining to threaten biodiversity. There is concern about major extinction of life forms. The IUCN (the Internation Union for the Conservation of Nature) reports 1 in 8 birds, 1 in 4 mammals and 1 in 3 of amphibian species are under threat. This threat can be addressed in cities by fostering vegetation, including roof gardens (German and Swiss legislation has required all buildings with flat roofs to be greened (i.e. vegetated) since the 1980s for new-build and renovation). And also by the development of public gardens and open space. Other simple measures include preventing the paving over of front gardens to create car-parking areas, or if this is to be permitted then prescribing (as in Denmark) the laying of two-track paving to accommodate car wheels with planting between.

Maintenance techniques in public areas can avoid the use of both insecticides and herbicides; a policy switch from cutting grass short to the cultivation of long meadow grass soon leads to benefits in terms of burgeoning insect populations. Woodland development, changes in agricultural practice and the re-creation of wetland areas can also promote biodiversity. Planning for ecological corridors can permit the movement of flora and fauna across the landscape as they respond to climate change.

Biodiversity Action Plans (BAPs) are a formal way of representing such action. BAPs are a response to the UN Convention on Biological Diversity of 1992. They involve a survey of the existing biological diversity, assessment of the conservation status of species and setting targets for conservation and finally setting in place the budgets and management which will achieve them.

The fostering of habitat is key to the survival of many species. The area of wildflower meadow and unimproved grassland in the United Kingdom has fallen to 2 per cent of its level in the 1930s, with a consequent loss of butterfly-rich habitats. There have been collapses in bird species populations, such as the house sparrow in London, due to urban habitat change. Internationally, there is widespread concern about the decline in the bee population because of the critical function it performs as a plant pollinator.

ECOLOGICAL FOOTPRINT

One consequence of the growth of the human population is an increase in net ecological footprint. The latter term is the measure of demand for natural capital expressed as global hectares per person. (gha). Natural capital is the stock of natural ecosystems yielding a continuing flow of valuable ecosystem goods or services. For example, a population of trees yields a flow of new trees, a flow that is indefinitely sustainable. Since the flow of services from ecosystems requires that they function as whole systems, the resilience and diversity of the system are important components of natural capital. One obvious example of loss of natural capital was the failure of the Newfoundland cod fishing grounds in the early 1990s due to overfishing and the ending of what had been the richest, most productive cod fishery in the world. It has still not recovered.

The global average productive area per person was 1.8gha. In 2007, according to the Global Footprint Network's Living Planet Report (2010), the US footprint was 8.0gha/person, Switzerland was 7.51 gha/person, and the Chinese footprint was 2.12 gha/person. China was just then moving into deficit. Overall human population with its current demands is exceeding the carrying capacity of the planet.

One challenge is that of reorganising the way developed countries consume the Earth's resources. The other is to find ways in which the growing populations of the world's megacities can be housed sustainably. But what has all of this got to do with landscape architecture? After all, it is only a small profession and can hardly determine population growth or seriously reduce our economic dependence on hydrocarbons on its own. Nonetheless, it can play its part in helping societies adjust to a low-carbon economy.

New models for sustainable urban development need to be explored for growing Asian, African and South American megacities; one answer might lie in the *barridas, bidonvilles* or slums that most planners and city authorities wish to remove because inhabitants are squatters and lack land tenure; while the land can be developed for commercial and high-priced housing. Those arguing for the survival of the Dharavi slum in Mumbai in India (where *Slumdog Millionaire* was filmed) or Korail in Dhaka in Bangladesh quote the rebuilding of Tokyo after 1945 or the rebuilding of Kobe after the 1985 earthquake as models for self-build redevelopment. In the Korail slum, city authorities wish to remove housing for 100,000 people and replace it with Western-style apartment blocks for 40,000. In Japan the local authorities provided infrastructure and the inhabitants put the buildings up themselves. Following this argument the critical thing for slums is to grant land tenure and provide basic services – water, sewerage, and power supply. Improve slums: don't demolish them.

CLIMATE CHANGE

Climate change is a trigger for all sorts of stresses we place on the Earth's resources and ecosystems. Growth of population, urbanization and humans' overall effect on the land are unbalancing. Global warming fundamentally impacts on our landscape and its ecosystems in ways we may judge as benign or adverse. For instance, northern Europe will see increased crop production due to the increase in temperatures, but there will be increased storms with consequent flash flooding. On current Intergovernmental Panel of Climate Change (IPCC) estimates, if there is a more than 2°C rise in average temperatures, southern Europe will experience lower rainfall and suffer desertification (two-thirds of Spain would become desert) and generally there are increasing sea level rises. There are vegetation changes and increased human death rates due to high temperature stress for the old, the ill and the young and the malaria-carrying Aedes mosquito will spread across Europe.

NATURAL CATASTROPHE COSTS

Two industries take climate change very very seriously: the insurance market and tourism: fiscal safety and sun are both things we crave. For example, look at the world's largest reinsurance group's Münchener Rück AG website www.munichre.com on the rise in insurance losses between 1980–2007 caused by natural catastrophe, due to, for instance, loss of coastal homes caused by sea flood and river flood disasters. Natural catastrophes are of concern.

To quote Münchener Rück:

Economic losses due to natural catastrophes rose faster than economic activity (e.g. due to population growth, globalization)	+	human-made climatic changes and development of new risk	+	increase of human-made disasters and development of new risk	+	Increased globalization and interdependency of risk	=	Rising demand for non-life insurance.

So for the insurance market, climate change is both a problem and an opportunity. However, for those no longer able to insure their home against loss due to coastal retreat these changes can be a financial disaster. Insurers measure the effects of climate change and charge a price on it. A price we cannot afford according to the *Stern Review*.

The *Stern Review on the Economics of Climate Change* of 2006 by economist Lord Stern (and former chief economic advisor to the Treasury) for the British government discusses the effect of climate change and global warming on the world economy. It argues that 1 per cent of global gross domestic product (GDP) per annum is required in order to avoid the worst effects of climate change.

It concludes that we cannot afford not to tackle climate change. The military also take climate change seriously: for instance the British Ministry of Defence's Development, Concepts and Doctrine Centre (DCDC) think tank's 'horizon-scanning' Strategic Trends Programme which forecasts world trends to 2040 'gives a detailed consideration of how climate change, global inequality, population growth, resource scarcity and the shifting balance of global power will transform the strategic context and create persistent, complex, global challenges'.

ECOLOGICAL FOOTPRINT

Ecological footprint, global hectares (gha) per person is a measure of demand for natural capital. The Earth's biocapacity is 2.1 gha/ person.

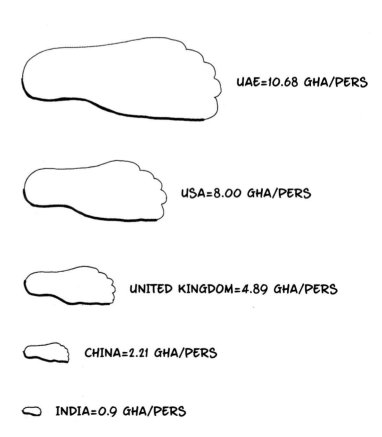

UAE=10.68 GHA/PERS

USA=8.00 GHA/PERS

UNITED KINGDOM=4.89 GHA/PERS

CHINA=2.21 GHA/PERS

INDIA=0.9 GHA/PERS

Korail, Dhaka, Bangladesh

Transforming a slum into a paradise

Landscape architect Khondaker Hasibul Kabir lives in Korail, a 49ha slum with a population of 120,000 people on the Banani Lake in the centre of Dhaka, the capital of Bangladesh. Dhaka had a population of over 16 million in 2011 of whom upwards of 3 million lived in slums. Dhaka is said to be the world's fastest-growing megacity. Bamboo structures built over the water line the shore between Gulshan Lake and Banani Lake.

Kabir studied landscape architecture at the University of Sheffield and on graduation in 2005 returned to Dhaka. He began work at BRAC University in the Department of Architecture. Seeking affordable accommodation in central Dhaka and being professionally interested in flood-prone rural areas, he looked for a home in Korail and moved in with Fourkan and Nasima Pevez in 2007. He helped the family plant trees and herbage in the surrounding area and created an open-air meeting place for local residents on a bamboo platform over the water. The Pevez family recycle their kitchen waste for compost and encourage other locals to plant their yards. They spread seeds on lakeside margins and have inspired their neighbours to do the same in order to

try to turn a slum into the beginnings of a sustainable urban paradise. On 9 April 2012, with one day's notice, the Dhaka City Corporation authorities began forced evictions of this vibrant community, who were living on state-owned land. They began clearing homes on Gulshan Lake where some of the capital's poorest people lived, homes that face wealthy, Western-style housing all around. The city authorities plan to build apartments on the sides of the lake. There are major concerns about this – the demolition of sustainable, low-impact homes for 100,000 people which work with the lakes, and the building of unsustainable, Western-style, high-rise apartments for 40,000 middle-class inhabitants in this city of flooding.

As we write the evictions have been temporarily halted by court order.

A. This bamboo platform serves as a community meeting place.
B. View across the lake showing the stilted construction over the water.
C. The Pevez family home.
D. Across the lake is more expensive housing.
E. A place for children to learn.
F. Paradise but without security.
G. A bare and bleak environment transformed.

A

Climate change involves a rise in average temperatures and extreme weather conditions as well as sea level increases and flooding, and threats to the water supply. The response involves switching to a low-carbon economy and addressing energy production by harnessing wind, water and tidal power. Landscape architects in many Western European countries, led by the Danish, have advised on both onshore and offshore windpower generation and the location of wind farms through environmental assessment studies. Tidal barrages or surge barriers are on the agenda in some locations, including the Thames estuary in the UK; such a major change will affect the coastal landscape to protect against flooding but can result in loss of marine habitat and marshland.

A low-carbon economy also involves a reduction in the use of private cars in favour of public transport, cycling and walking. In the West, efforts to remodel the city around the motor car have proved dangerous and destructive. Cities should be for people to walk, trade, meet and mingle in, and the centrality of the automobile should be diminished. Most city streets are currently dominated by the car. Landscape architects can play a part in moving urban spaces away from car-based transport planning. The example of Copenhagen since the 1960s, where planning has favoured people over cars, shows a way to reverse this trend. Both Paris and London have seen increases in cycling and public transport use in the past 20 years, but at the same time cities in China have been moving in the opposite direction.

Efforts to ameliorate the effects of climate change need not be high-tech. Take the heat island effect in cities. Street tree planting provides shade and is a way of reducing high temperatures in the summer – high temperatures lead to both increased geriatric and perinatal death rates. Similarly SUDS (Sustainable Drainage Systems) are a way of dealing with threats of falling groundwater levels (necessary for vegetation growth) as well as reducing flood risk.

We referred above to urban heat island effect and how street tree shade in cities can reduce air temperature in the summer. Tree planting has wider environmental benefits, however. It can reduce air pollution by removing particulates, small solid particles that affect lung function and make it difficult to breathe. Trees also absorb gases such as carbon monoxide, nitrogen oxide and sulphur dioxide which can cause respiratory problems and increase asthma problems. Views of urban greenery have also been shown to improve mental well-being, not to mention encouraging exercise. In short, urban tree planting – at its most direct in the form of avenue tree planting – provides a healthier urban environment for humans as well as promoting biodiversity and a habitat for birds and other creatures.

HOW LANDSCAPE ARCHITECTS CAN CONTRIBUTE TO THE AMELIORATION OF THE EFFECTS OF CLIMATE CHANGE

A current checklist is:

- ecological corridors to promote migration of flora and fauna;
- water conservation;
- use of drought-tolerant, genetically diverse plants and changes in cultivation;
- shade structures (e.g. roadside trees) to promote human comfort, and ameliorate the urban heat island effect;
- urban tree planting to capture atmospheric dust;
- green roofs to slow surface water run-off and promote biodiversity;
- management of coastal retreat policies due to rising sea levels;
- agricultural and landscape restructuring as the tree line moves upwards;
- afforestation (the planting of new forests);
- promotion of recycling and composting;
- river basin management to cope with the loss of flood plains;
- soil conservation and soil carbon sink policy;
- promotion of cycling and walking in cities and elsewhere;
- promotion of wind farms and solar and hydroelectric energy, and network environmental assessment of energy distribution;
- environmental assessment and design of public transport including road, rail and bus transport;
- increase in the albedo of urban surface area (e.g. roofs and roads to improve reflectivity).

The last requires a little explanation: albedo is a measure of reflectivity on a low to high scale of 0–10 with 0 as black and 10 as white. Urbanization changes areas from vegetated green fields (about 5) to black roads and roofs. Avoidance of black asphalt, by planting roadside tree planting and green or vegetated roofs, are ways of raising the albedo of a city, increasing the reflectivity of the Earth's surface, reducing the absorption of solar heat, and thus reducing global warming.

A

B

C

D

A. Newly planted living wall showing supporting structure, Venlo Floriade 2012, the Netherlands.

B. Established vertical green wall planting, London.

C. Biodiverse brown roof at the Centre for Alternative Technology, Machynlleth, Wales: a brown roof using local subsoil or rubble which seeds itself naturally and promotes a rich diversity of habitat.

D. Extensive green roof, Horniman Museum, London.

North Holland coastline, the Netherlands

Development in coastal dyke defences

Coastal protection in Holland is changing, and one project showing current ideas in flood protection is the work of the multi-disciplinary practice Arcadis in Province North Holland, to the north-west of Alkmaar. This is a study of options for strengthening 6km of coastline, between Hondsbossche and Pettemer Zeewering; behind the coastline are nature reserves and 400-year-old polders.

This stretch of coastal dyke is a weak link in the North Holland flood defences, and there is a national programme to strengthen these weak stretches with the aim of upgrading flood protection and improving the environment. One plank of the programme is community involvement in the designs.

Arcadis developed alternative solutions, based on an analysis of the landscape, ranging from raising dykes to sand nourishment and allowing for more overspill. Along with these alternatives, they developed design proposals for improving spatial quality with an emphasis on landscape and cultural heritage,

recreation and tourism, liveability and nature development. Visualizations were key to communicating the plans. The conclusion has been that an integrated approach is the preferred solution, strengthening the defences using sand nourishment on the shoreline because it offers a flexible approach to coastal protection. It gives benefits in the long term as well, with possibilities for nature conservation, improved accessibility and new beaches for recreation and tourism, while protecting the heritage of the polders behind. This sustainable solution is in keeping with the current strategies with dealing with Dutch coast defences and can count on community support.

As landscape architect at Arcadis Gertjan Jobse says, this is part of the response to how climate change affects Dutch sea defences, 'landscape is intrinsically dynamic, constantly in motion.' Here he is creating a new coastal seascape which responds to change.

A

A. After-view, coast with sand nourishment and beach creation.
B. Bird's-eye view of present situation with engineering dyke and low, wide groynes.
C. Bird's-eye view of dyke raised higher and wider using conventional engineering response and groynes maintained.
D. Flood response using overspill techniques with groynes retained and reinforcement with rock structures.
E. Dyke reinforced by sand nourishment. Bird's-eye view high tide.
F. Coastal dyke and present situation.

Recycling and everyday practice

There are increases in the costs of raw materials – timber, stone, metals, plastics – in view of world demand. Timber can be twice as expensive as plastic or polymer substitutes, but polymers use more energy in production and are based on hydrocarbon feedstocks. Recycling of materials is one way forward: reuse what you have, don't waste it. This is already common practice with metals, such as steel and aluminium, but is good practice with all materials. Century-old road kerbs can easily be reused, as can paving slabs in both stone and pre-cast concrete. There is a long tradition of reusing brickwork, but this is based on lime mortar being easy to remove. The switch to much stronger cement mortar since the early twentieth century has made this more difficult – so why not just switch back to lime mortar?

Half of the world's population are said to live in earth buldings (meaning mud brick and adobe); such traditional construction is low in embodied carbon and low in embodied energy compared with fired clay or sand bricks.

In the UK it is normal practice to bed unit paving, whether stone slabs or brick blocks, on 150mm of concrete foundations. Such construction is high in embodied carbon, high in embodied energy, expensive and cracks easily. It is rigid and wrong. By contrast, it is normal in many continental European countries to bed brick and stone paving on sand. The UK should adopt a similar practice. Landscape architects should always question what they do.

Avoid use of peat-based composts; peat is a valuable carbon sink. Instead promote soil fertility and water retention by making compost on site. Recycling is not just important in the initial capital works of a project, it should be built into the ongoing development. The opportunities for embedding recycling and sustainability into landscape architecture practice are endless. The above examples may seem trivial but cumulatively they can have a dramatic effect.

Landscape architects need to consider the environmental implications of all their design decisions and to explore sustainable alternatives.

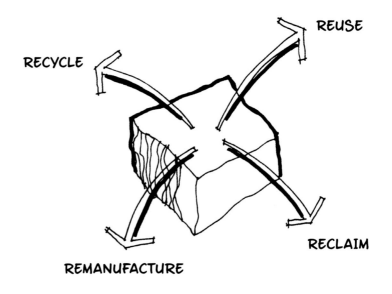

RECYCLE   REUSE   REMANUFACTURE   RECLAIM

A

B

C

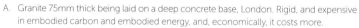

A. Granite 75mm thick being laid on a deep concrete base, London. Rigid, and expensive in embodied carbon and embodied energy, and, economically, it costs more.

B. Often when poorly detailed the concrete base will lead to cracking in the decorative surface, Paris.

C. Reclaimed concrete foundations broken up and reused as stepping stones, Venlo Floriade 2012, the Netherlands.

D. Pre-cast concrete paving prior to laying, Paris.

E. In situ concrete is prone to cracking even on high profile projects, UNESCO Noguchi Garden, Paris.

F. Large-scale pre-cast concrete paving units laid in a simple grid form, Venlo Floriade 2012, the Netherlands.

G. Bridge of recycled scaffolding planks, Wilde Weelde (Wild World) garden designed by Jasper Helmantel, Venlo Floriade 2012, the Netherlands.

H. In the urban public realm coordination of below-ground services is crucial to avoid this situation in Belfast.

I. Simple, coordinated detailing using pre-cast concrete walls and paving units all loose laid on a compacted sub-base.

Final thoughts

These challenges are all opportunities for the future of landscape architecture. We need to change the way we live, to realize that the free market has its limits, that commons in its economic sense should be valued. We need to act as stewards for our world which increasingly is formed and dominated by human activity: we need to treat our planet with care. It is for the landscape architects of the next 50 years, for whom this book was written, to seize them. Let us end with a further quotation from the Philadelphia Declaration of 1966 with which we began this chapter:

'There is no "single solution" but groups of solutions carefully related one to another. There is no one-shot cure, nor single-purpose panacea, but the need for collaborative solutions. A key to solving the environmental crisis comes from the field of landscape architecture, a profession dealing with the interdependence of environmental processes.'

Landscape architecture needs to respond to climate change, and its effects ameliorated, by for instance:

A. Boulevard Henri IV, Paris, street trees lower temperature in hot weather, promote wildlife and trees trap particulates in the air.

B. Extensive planted roofs slow water run-off and contribute to a sustainable drainage system (SUDS), so avoiding flooding.

C. Lime tree-lined Royal Avenue in Chelsea, London with light gravel paving, which raises the albedo (or reflectivity) of the city.

D. Trees growing out of Johnson's Draw Dock Millwall, London.

E. Green roofs raise albedo, provide habitat for wildlife and slow water run-off.

F. Living walls are all the rage, like this one in Trafalgar Square, London. They provide habitat but at a huge cost of constant irrigation and care. A couple of self-clinging climbing plants can cover a wall equally well.

G. Vertical gardens, like these in Barcelona, create green where otherwise there is no life.

H. Vegetated swale (basically a wide, permeable ditch, which is dry when it is not raining), part of a SUDS, Venlo Floriade 2012, the Netherlands.

Glossary

Autobahn German, 'motorway'.

Beaux-Arts Late nineteenth-century style characterized by symmetry, axial planning, rich ornamentation, and a grand scale. From the *Ecole des Beaux Arts,* the chief architecture and art school in Paris of the time.

Bill of quantities A documented list describing the measurement of each item of a construction contract – e.g. length, area, volume or weight – so that it may be priced as a part of the tender process.

Biodiversity The variety of plant and animal life, in the world or in a particular habitat.

Biome A complex of ecosystems that relate to a particular climate, and environment – for example, a tropical forest, grassland, or a coral reef.

Biotope An area of uniform environmental conditions providing a living place for a specific assemblage of plants and animals. The subject of a biotope is an ecological community.

Brutalism From French *béton brut,* 'rough concrete'. A form of Modernist architecture during the 1950s to the '70s typified by raw concrete structures.

Building Information Modelling (BIM) A virtual or digital resource that includes information of width, height and length (traditionally represented by plan, section, and elevation) in addition to specification, cost, time and other information.

Bundesgartenschau A German garden festival. Half a year in duration and years in preparation.

Capital value The worth of the land and buildings of a development.

Civil engineering Field of structural design that includes geotechnical, water resources, structural, marine, and materials engineering specialisms.

Climate change 'A change of climate which is attributed directly or indirectly to human activity that alters the composition of the global atmosphere and which is in addition to natural climate variability observed over comparable time periods.' – United Nations Framework Convention on Climate Change (UNFCCC) 1992.

Common goods Or Commons. In economics one of the four main types of goods. Examples include fish stocks in non-controlled, international waters, coal resources or forests, the atmosphere, seas and rivers, and climate change.

Competitive tendering A process through which contracts are awarded on the basis of competitive (usually secret) bidding by a number of bidders.

Completion Process at the end of a construction contract. It involves 'practical completion' (when the works are sufficiently complete to be used by the client but not necessarily complete in all the works); 'defects completion' at the end of the defects liability period during which the contractor is responsible for making good defects; 'legal completion' is when the final account is paid, legally this means that all parties to the contract have fulfilled their obligations.

Conservation Protection, preservation, management, or restoration of historical, cultural, wildlife and natural resources such as urban areas, countryside, forests, soil, and water.

Conurbation Group of towns, villages and other urban areas that grow together to merge into one continuous urban area.

Cost benefit evaluation Systematic process for comparing benefits and costs of a project, by estimating the costs of each option and comparing them with the forecast benefits to determine whether it is suitable for investment. Also known as cost benefit analysis.

Cost estimate A forecast of the cost of a project calculated on the basis of the current project information (such as floor area of building or extent of site) and precedent costs.

Cost estimator See Quantity surveyor.

Cost planning Cost planning predicts or estimates how much a project will cost to build, the variables are the quality, the quantities, time scale and embodied carbon or other aspects of sustainability.

Cultural landscape A landscape modified by humans.

Dataset A collection of related but discrete sets of information open to manipulation as a unit by a computer.

Detail proposals Describe materials, techniques, and standards of workmanship sufficient to submit for statutory approvals (e.g. building regulations) and to obtain the client's approval for the next stage of work.

Development surveyor Responsible for planning and development, including assessment of land and property use requirements and development and regeneration appraisal and related planning implementation processes. Also known as planning and development surveyor.

Ecological footprint The impact of a person or community on the environment, expressed as the amount of land required to sustain their use of natural resources, measured in global hectares per person.

Ecology The study of plant, animal and human communities and their relationships with each other and with the environment.

Ecosystem A community of organisms that interact with each other and with their physical and chemical environment.

EIA Environmental Impact Assessment.

Embodied carbon i) the sum of all the energy required to manufacture goods or services, ii) the sum of all the energy required to deliver a product, including the energy used in maintaining it, demolishing and recycling it. It can be expressed as carbon kg CO_2 per kg.

Embodied energy The energy required to extract, process, transport, install, maintain and dispose of a product or component; expressed in millijoules per kg (MJ/kg).

Environmental assessment A procedure to ensure the environmental implications of decisions are taken into account before the decisions for a development project, plan or policy are made.

European directive European Union legislation that determines particular results for member states to achieve, but does not determine the means of achieving those results. A framework directive establishes aims over a broader field but, again, does not specify the means by which they should be achieved.

Freehold Permanent and absolute ownership of land or property, with freedom to dispose of it.

Functionalism A principle of Modernism that the form of the building should be dictated by its function. The phrase 'Form ever follows function' was used by the Chicago skyscraper architect Louis Sullivan in 1896.

Gaia theory Hypothesis proposed by scientist James Lovelock that the biosphere contributes to the stability of the planet's physical processes, such as temperature, ocean water salt levels, etc., allowing life to flourish.

Garden festival An exhibition of garden design and horticulture for a season (usually six months) based on the example of the German *Bundesgartenschauen*. In the Netherlands they are held every ten years and are known as *Floriade*.

Genplan Masterplan, or general plan, an abbreviation of the Russian for 'General Plan for the Reconstruction of Moscow'.

Geomorphology The study of landforms and the processes that shape them.

Green belt The designation of land around certain cities and large built-up areas, which aims to keep it permanently open or largely undeveloped.

Green wedges Greenways or open space of wedge form which radiate from a city centre, as in the Copenhagen Finger Plan of 1947 or Moscow's Genplan of 1935. Also open land separating settlements.

Habitat The natural home or environment where an organism or a community of organisms lives, including all living and non-living factors and conditions.

Heempark A Dutch park that includes native vegetation types and species, used in the teaching of natural history.

Historicist In reference to landscape architecture, using historical styles or motifs.

Irrigation Watering by artificial means, as by sprinkler, drip, or basin flooding or other form of surface or sub-surface irrigation.

Land consolidation Re-arrangement of land plots and their ownership. usually undertaken to form larger and more productive land holdings.

Landscape garden A garden laid out to suggest the effect of natural scenery.

Landscape planning '... an activity concerned with reconciling competing land uses while protecting natural processes and significant cultural and natural resources' – Ervin H. Zube.

Landscape urbanism A theory of planning and design for urbanism proposing that *landscape*, rather than *architecture*, is capable of organizing the city and developing urban living.

Landscape Visual Impact Assessment (LVIA) See Visual Impact Assessment.

Licensure The granting of a license for a profession to practice, especially in the US, where it is granted at state level with examinations supervised by the Council of Landscape Architectural Registration Boards (CLARB). Elsewhere the equivalent is **registration**, although frequently this is on the basis of education.

Linear park Parks that follow a linear route through the city, e.g. the Emerald Necklace in Boston.

Locus The position or place where something occurs or is situated.

Low-carbon economy An economy that minimizes output of greenhouse gas emissions, and specifically refers to carbon dioxide as a marker for all greenhouse gases.

Mechanical and electrical engineer (M & E engineer) Role with a wide range of engineering responsibilities including the analysis, design, and fabrication, supply and maintenance of mechanical systems. In relation to construction and building services their responsibilities include the design of the mechanical, electrical and public health system, including underground services and electrical systems. Also known as Building Services Engineering.

Megacity A city typically with a population of more than ten million inhabitants.

Modernism Early twentieth-century artistic movement marked by a rejection of ornament and the figurative, using simple forms and symmetrical layout. It was also a response to technological and functional change and embraced new materials and structures. In landscape architecture the stylistic markers are an asymmetrical layout and simple architectural form, whether of structures, paving or planting, together with biomorphic pools.

Municipal park Open space, or park for public use maintained by a town council.

National park A reserve or protected area of natural, semi-natural, or developed land.

Natural capital Includes i) the stock of natural assets in their role of providing natural resource inputs and environmental services for economic production; ii) the renewable and non-renewable resources that enter the production process and satisfy consumption needs; iii) environmental assets that have amenity and productive use; and iv) natural features, such as the ozone layer, that are essential for supporting life.

New Town Particularly one of 28 new towns in the UK built to accommodate those displaced by slum clearance in the 1950s. Japan also built 30 new towns from the 1960s. In the Netherlands new towns were associated with polder reclamation.

New Urbanism A current in urban design since the 1980s that promotes mixed-use, walkable neighbourhoods. The movement has been active in the US as a reaction to car-based, post-war development that has single-use zoning, suburban housing and out-of-town shopping centres.

NGO Non-governmental organization.

Orthogonal Ninety-degree plan form.

Particulates Fine airborne particles with a diameter of 10 micrometres or less. They are formed by natural (volcanoes, forest fires, dust storms, salt water spray, etc.) and human-made sources (vehicles, fossil fuels, industrial processes, etc.). Their effects are reduced by vegetation.

Plant community Group of plant species in a defined area that constitutes a uniform patch compared with adjacent vegetation.

Plot layout Layout plan that shows the main features, such as roads, building and building parcels or plots.

Polder Area of land enclosed by a dyke or raised embankment by which water from river or sea flooding is excluded and drained artificially, characteristic of the Netherlands and other low-lying coastal and river delta areas.

Polder reclamation The process of winning agricultural land or land for other purposes by creating a polder. In the Netherlands this involves building an enclosing dyke, a drainage system of canals, pumping water to a set level, establishing a soil structure by planting *Juncus* reed for some years, and then farming the land. Pumping is maintained for the life of the polder and permits accurate control of the groundwater table.

Post-industrial Refers to projects on former industrial sites that do not eradicate traces of industry but rather incorporate them.

Postmodern Movement that developed playful, decorated, symbolic and allegorical designs and formed a reaction to **Modernism**. In landscape design it dates from the late 1970s.

Precast Refers to concrete that has been manufactured or formed at a site away from the final construction location.

Primary forest A forest largely undisturbed by human activity. Also known as virgin forest, first-growth forest.

Private sector The part of the economy that is not state-owned, and is operated by companies for profit.

Production information Documentation in the form of drawings, specifications, schedules and quantities that describes a proposed construction project. Increasingly it is communicated and coordinated using Building Information Modelling (BIM).

Professional fees Payment for consultancy work done by a professional; they do not include expenses.

Propagation Reproduction of plants by seeds, cuttings, grafting, layering, micropropagation, etc. Seed propagation involves sexual reproduction with consequent genetic variation, while vegetative reproduction such as cuttings and grafting, produces a genetically identical clone of the parent plant.

Prospect An extensive sight or view; the view of the landscape from any given position.

Public open space (POS) Open space accessible to the public, both land and water areas providing for sport and outdoor recreation including public parks and gardens, squares and civic spaces, nature reserves and green corridors, sports fields, playgrounds, allotments, cemeteries and churchyards.

Quantity surveyor (QS) Quantity surveyors estimate the construction cost and offer advice on project management, procurement and contract management.

Redevelopment area Areas where existing structures and buildings are largely demolished because they are out of use or inappropriately used (in the view of the planners) and therefore demolished to make way for new transport links and building development.

Registration The granting of professional status and the right to practise by means of enlisting on a state register. An international equivalent of the American licensure.

Ribbon development Linear development of houses and settlements alongside main roads or tramways, radiating from an urban centre. A cause of urban sprawl.

Rigid paving A type of paving made on site using a rigid or relatively inflexible material, or made of units laid on an inflexible foundation, such as in situ concrete.

Romanticism Cultural movement that emerged in the mid eighteenth century linked with a democratization of ideas and power, belief in liberty and the power of the imagination, and in contrast to the rationalism of the Enlightenment. Romanticism in landscape gardening was typified by the picturesque English landscape garden, its attempted re-creation of wild or 'natural' features and the use of gothic, rustic, and classical references and motifs.

SEA Strategic Environmental Assessment.

Secondary forest Forests that regenerate largely through natural processes after significant removal or disturbance of the original forest vegetation by human or natural causes at a single point in time or over an extended period. Their structure and/or canopy species composition are majorly different from primary forests. Also known as second-growth forest.

Sieve mapping A constraints and opportunities process in landscape planning that builds up a number of geographical layers to produce a visual representation of areas that show potential for development.

Sketch scheme proposals Early design development proposals, for spatial arrangements, materials and appearance sufficient to obtain client's approval to proceed to the next stage of work.

Speculative developer Developer of a building or real estate who works without a pre-let lease or buyer arranged beforehand. Typically the ambition of a speculative developer might be short-term return with the aim of selling on the site.

Stormwater Excess rainfall or other precipitation (e.g. snow or ice melt), which, unable to soak into saturated land, runs off along the surface.

Strategic Environmental Assessment (SEA) A form of Environmental Assessment aiming to assess and guide policy, such as economic policy, promoted by the European Union Strategic Environmental Assessment Directive (2001).

Strategic planning Overall spatial plan for an area, showing the main lines or areas of development, change or conservation proposed. Also known as a vision plan.

Structural engineer Engineer who analyzes and designs structures that support or resist loads; these may include buildings and roads.

Succession Process of change in an ecosystem as one community establishes, modifies the habitat, and is replaced by another community until a stable climax is established, e.g. open water to fen or swamp, to marshland, to alder or willow carr, to oak-ash woodland.

Surveyor Professional who measures land in three dimensions and is fundamental to most planning, construction and development.

Sustainability The conservation of ecological balance by avoiding the depletion of natural resources.

Sustainable Drainage Systems (SUDS) Sustainable urban drainage systems – including green roofs, detention basins and swales – used to slow run-off from a built-up area in order to avoid flooding. Necessary because building development renders soil impermeable and increases surface water run-off.

Tender An offer to supply a service or product, or to carry out work for a contract; can also apply to an offer for professional services.

Theme park A commercial amusement park with rides orchestrated around themes or stories and with coordinated landscape, scene-setting, and ownership.

Urban design The design of towns and villages, including disposition and design of groups of buildings, of streets and public spaces, neighbourhoods and districts, and entire cities, to produce functional, attractive and sustainable urban areas.

Urban heat island Built-up areas that have higher average temperatures than surrounding undeveloped land. These occur because the materials in built-up areas are darker and retain more heat than vegetated countryside, and because of waste heat produced in developed areas.

Urban sprawl Pejorative term referring to the spreading of a city in uncontrolled, low-density development, often with cars as the main mode of transport.

Visual Impact Assessment The measurement and appraisal of the effects of a proposed development on the landscape and visual resource of the area. Also known as LVIA (Landscape Visual Impact Assessment).

Zone Of Theoretical Visibility (ZTV) The determination of the theoretical visibility of a development in the landscape measured by an analysis of the topography or contours of the area, theoretical because it does not allow for the restriction of views by trees, buildings, etc. ZTV identifies areas where a development cannot be seen, but not necessarily all of the extent of the non visibility. Also known as Zone of Visual Influence (ZVI).

Bibliography

Introduction

General guides and introductions.
- Foster, Kelleann, *Becoming a Landscape Architect: A Guide to Careers in Design,* John Wiley & Sons, 2009
- Ormsbee Simonds, John & Starke, Barry, *Landscape Architecture: A Manual of Land Planning and Design,* McGraw-Hill Professional, fifth edition 2013
- Rottle, Nancy & Yocom, Ken, *Basics Landscape Architecture 02: Ecological Design,* AVA Publishing, 2011
- Waterman, Tim, *The Fundamentals of Landscape Architecture,* AVA Publishing, 2009
- Waterman, Tim & Wall, Ed, *Basics Landscape Architecture 01: Urban Design,* AVA Publishing, 2009

Biographies
- McHarg, Ian, *Quest for Life: An Autobiography,* John Wiley & Sons, 1996
- Stinson, Kathy, *A Love Every Leaf: The Life of Landscape Architect Cornelia Hahn,* Oberlander, Tundra Books, 2008
- Thompson, Ian, *Ecology, Ecology, Community and Delight: An Inquiry into Values in Landscape Architecture: Sources of Value in Landscape Architecture,* Routledge, 1999

Magazines
- ASLA Landscape Architecture Magazine http://landscapearchitecturemagazine.org/
- *Bund der Deutscher Landschaftsarchitekten* (BDLA) *Garten + Landschaft* http://www.garten-landschaft.de/
- Landscape Institute's Landscape http://www.landscapeinstitute.org/publications/landscapejournal.php
- Topos (http://www.toposmagazine.com/)
- 'Scape http://www.scapemagazine.com/about.html
- Greenplaces http://www.green-places.co.uk/
- Landscape Architecture Foundation LandscapeOnline Weekly. http://www.landscapeonline.com/products/listing.php?id=11024

Monographs
- de Jong, Erik & Bertram, Christian, *Michael Van Gessel: Landscape Architect,* NAI Publishers, 2008
- Saunder, William, *Designed Ecologies: the Landscape Architecture of Kingjian Yu,* Birkhäuser, 2012

Practice websites
- AECOM: http://www.aecom.com/What+We+Do/Design+and+Planning/Practice+Areas/Landscape+Architecture+and+Urban+Design
- Belt Collins: http://www.beltcollins.com/#/home
- Building Design Partnership: http://www.bdp.com/en/Services/Landscape-Architecture/
- Atelier Dreiseitl: http://www.dreiseitl.net/
- Field Operations: http://www.fieldoperations.net/
- Michael van Gessel: http://www.michaelvangessel.com/
- George Hargreaves: http://www.hargreaves.com/
- Land Use Consultants: http://www.landuse.co.uk/
- SWA: http://www.swagroup.com/
- Agence Ter: http://www.agenceter.com/
- Turenscape: http://www.turenscape.com/english/
- West 8: http://www.west8.nl/
- Kim Wilkie: http://www.kimwilkie.com/

General landscape architecture websites
- www.gardenvisit.com/
- *The Field* http://thefield.asla.org/
- http://www.land8lounge.com/
- *The Dirt* http://dirt.asla.org/

Salary surveys
- http://www.bls.gov/ooh/Architecture-and-Engineering/Landscape-architects.htm
- http://www.bls.gov/oes/current/oes171012.htm#nat
- http://asla.org/ContentDetail.aspx?id=11346
- http://www.aila.org.au/surveys/salary.htm
- http://www.landscapeinstitute.org/news/index.php/news_articles/view/how_much_do_landscape_architects_earn/

Definitions of landscape architecture
- http://www.iflaonline.org/index.php?Itemid=42&view=article&option=com_content&id=37 http://www.asla.org/ContentDetail.aspx?id=12200&PageTitle=Education&RMenuId=54 http://www.asla.org/uploadedFiles/CMS/Government_Affairs/Public_Policies/Licensure_Definition_of_Practice.pdf
- http://www.bdla.de/seite102.htm
- http://www.landscapeinstitute.org.uk/PDF/Contribute/Landscape_Institute_Royal_Charter_Revised_Version_July_2008.pdf

Chapter 1 The History of Landscape Architecture

- Barlow Rogers, Elizabeth, *Landscape Design: A Cultural and Architectural History,* Harry N. Abrams, 2001
- Goode, Patrick, Lancaster, Michael, & Jellicoe, Susan and Geoffrey, The *Oxford Companion to Gardens,* Oxford University Press, 2001
- Jellicoe, Geoffrey and Susan, *Landscape of Man: Shaping the Environment From Prehistory to the Present Day,* Thames & Hudson, 1995
- Turner, Tom, *European Gardens: History, Philosophy and Design,* Routledge, 2011
- — *Asian Gardens: History, Beliefs and Design,* Routledge, 2010

Garden design
- Buchan, Ursula, *The English Garden,* Frances Lincoln, 2006
- Dixon-Hunt, John, *The Picturesque Garden* in Europe, Thames & Hudson, 2004
- Keswick, Maggie, *Chinese Garden,* Frances Lincoln, 2003
- Richardson, Tim, *The Arcadian Friends, Inventing the English Landscape Garden,* Bantam Press, 2007
- Siren, Osvald, *Gardens of China,* Dumbarton Oaks, 1990
- Woodbridge, Kenneth, *Princely Gardens: Origins and Development of the French Formal Style,* Thames & Hudson, 1986

The growth of landscape architecture as a profession
- Aldous, Tony, Clouston, Brian & Alexander, Rosemary *Landscape by Design,* Heinemann, 1979
- Beveridge, Charles, *Frederick Law Olmsted: Designing the American Landscape,* Universe, 2005
- Brown, Jane, *The Modern Garden,* Thames & Hudson, 2000
- Hauxner, Malene, *Open to the Sky,* Arkitektens Forlag, 2003
- Landscape Architecture Europe Foundation, *Fieldwork,* Birkhäuser, 2006
  — *On Site,* Birkhäuser, 2009
  — *In Touch,* Birkhäuser, 2012
- Lund, Annemarie, *Guide to Danish Landscape Architecture 1000-2003,* Arkitektens Forlag, 1997
- Newton, Norman T., *Design on the Land: the Development of Landscape Architecture,* Belknap Press, 1971
- Racine, Michel (ed.), *Createurs de Jardins et de Paysages en France du XIXe siècle au XXIe Siècle,* Actes Sud, 2002
- Reh, Wouter & Steenbergen, Clemens, *Metropolitan Landscape Architecture – Urban Parks And Landscapes,* Thoth, 2012
- Uekoetter, Frank, *The Green and the Brown, a History of Conservation in Nazi Germany,* Cambridge University Press, 2006

- http://www.FrederickLawOlmsted.com/
- http://www.olmsted.org/home

Changing priorities: ecology, biodiversity and sustainability
- Dinep, Claudia & Schwab, Kristin, *Sustainable Site Design: Criteria, Process, and Case Studies for Integrating Site and Region in Landscape Design,* John Wiley & Sons, 2010
- Gillett, M., *Ecosystems,* Hodder Education, 2005
- Rottle, Nancy & Yocom, Ken, *Basics Landscape Architecture 02: Ecological Design,* AVA Publishing, 2011
- Schulze, Ernst-Detlef, Beck, Erwin & Müller-Hohenstein, Klaus, *Plant Ecology,* Springer, 2005
- Turner, Monica G., Gardner, Robert H. & O'Neil, Robert V., *Landscape Ecology in Theory and Practice: Pattern and Process,* Springer, 2001

- American Society of Landscape Architects, *Sustainable Design Resource Guides and Toolkit*, which range from *Green Infrastructure* to *Maximising the Benefits of Plants* or to *Climate Change*. Each has recommended reading and online resources, see http://www.asla.org/ContentDetail.aspx?id=29222

Chapter 1 case studies
- Painshill Park, Surrey, UK
  http://www.painshill.co.uk/
- Emscher Park IBA, Ruhr Valley, Germany
  http://en.landschaftspark.de/the-park/evolution/iba
  http://www.iba.nrw.de/main.htm
- Ijsselmeerpolders, the Netherlands
  http://www.flevoland.nl/english/

Chapter 2 Beginning a Project

The brief, types of client and fees
- Clamp, Hugh, *Landscape Professional Practice*, Gower Publishing, 1999
- Knox, Paul and Ozolins, Peter (ed.) *The Design Professionals and the Built Environment, an Introduction*, John Wiley & Sons, 2000
- Tennant, Rachel, Garmony, N. & Winsch, C., *Professional Practice for Landscape Architects*, Architectural Press, 2002

- Landscape Institute guidelines http://www.landscapeinstitute.org/publications/downloads.php. Among them is *Landscape Architecture: Elements and Areas of Practice – an Educational Framework*, 2012.
  Appointing a Chartered Landscape Architect: Guidelines for Best Value, 2003 is a guideline for clients. *Engaging a Landscape Consultant. Guidance for Clients on Fees*, 2002 describes the various fee arrangements possible in some detail.
  Landscape Institute, *Pathway to Chartership* http://www.pathwaytochartership.org/login
  Landscape Institute *Guidebook to the Pathway to Chartership*, 2010 http://www.landscapeinstitute.org.uk/PDF/Contribute/LI_Pathway_Handbook.pdf http://fidic.org/bookshop
- A useful introduction to common goods is http://dlc.dlib.indiana.edu/dlc/
- American Society of Landscape Architects (ASLA) professional practice website area, http://www.asla.org/ResourceLanding.aspx equally aimed at supporting those in practice.
- ASLA, *Standard Form Contracts for Professional Services* http://www.asla.org/ContentDetail.aspx?id=14888
- *Bund Deutscher Landschaftsarchitekten* (BDLA) has fee guidance and professional service guidance for its members on http://www.bdla.de/seite95.htm
- *Nederlanse Vereniging voor Tuin en Landschaparchitectur* (NVTL) website http://www.nvtl.nl/service/beroepsondersteuning hosts the DNR or *De Nieuwe Regeling*: 2011, (literally the new rules) the standard Dutch form of professional agreement course in Dutch and English.
- The Australian Institute of Landscape Architects (AILA) refers its members, see http://www.aila.org.au/practicenotes/ to AS4122-2010, *General Conditions of Contract for Engagement of Consultants* published by Standards Australia (ref. http://infostore.saiglobal.com/store/details.aspx?ProductID=143930
- A consultancy agreement based on engineering practice is the Client-Consultant Agreement (White Book), fourth edition 2006, of the International Federation of Civil Engineers (FIDIC)

Site survey
- Beer, Anne R. & Higgins, Catherine, *Environmental Planning for Site Development, A Manual for Sustainable Local Planning and Design*, E and FN Spon, 2000
- Ormsbee Simonds, John & Starke, Barry, *Landscape Architecture: A Manual for Land Planning and Design*, McGraw-Hill, 2006
- Rubenstein, Harvey M., *A Guide to Site Planning and Landscape Construction*, John Wiley & Sons, 1996

Chapter 2 case studies
- Westergasfabriek Park, Amsterdam, the Netherlands
  http://www.westergasfabriek.nl/en/westergasfabriek-en/park
  http://courses.umass.edu/latour/Netherlands/varro/index.html

- Central Park, New York City
  Barlow Rogers, E., Cramer, E.M., Heintz, J. L., Kelly, B., Winslow, P. N. & Berendt, J., *Rebuilding Central Park: A Management and Restoration Plan*, MIT Press, 1987
  http://www.centralparknyc.org/
- Thames Barrier Park, London
  http://www.arup.com/_assets/_download/download17.pdf
  Holden, Robert, 'Park and Pride', *Architects' Journal* 12/7/2001 pp. 24-33 http://www.architectsjournal.co.uk/buildings/park-and-pride/182988.article
  Racine, Michel, *Allain Provost – Landscape Architect / Paysagiste: Invented Landscapes / Paysages Inventés - '64–'04*, Ulmer Eugen Verlag, 2005

Chapter 3 The Design Process

Revealing the site
- Book, Norman K., *Basic Elements of Landscape Architecture Design*, Elsevier, 1983
- Lynch, Kevin & Hack, Gary, *Site Planning*, MIT, 1984

The principles of design
- Bachelard, Gaston, *Poetics of Space*, Beacon Press, 1994
- Berger, John, *Ways of Seeing*, Penguin, 1972
- Critchlow, Keith & Allen, Jon, *Drawing Geometry: A Primer of Basic Forms for Artists, Designers and Architects*, Floris Books, 2007
- Holtzschue, Linda, *Understanding Colour*, John Wiley & Sons, 2002
- Itten, Johannes, *The Elements of Color*, John Wiley & Sons, 1970
- Olsen, Scott, *The Golden Section*, Wooden Books, 2009
- Porter, Tom, & Goodman, Sue, *Design Primer for Architects, Graphic Designers and Artists*, Butterworth-Heinemann, 1989
- Pye, David, *The Nature & Aesthetics of Design*, A & C Black Ltd, 2000
- Ryan, Mark, *Geometry for Dummies*, John Wiley & Sons, 2008
- de Sausmarez, Maurice & Kepes, G., *Basic Design: The Dynamics of Visual Form*, McGraw-Hill, 1990

Environmental design
- Beck, Travis, *Principles of Ecological Landscape Design*, Island Press, 2012
- Ching, Francis, *Architecture, Form, Space and Order*, John Wiley & Sons, 2007
- Hough, Michael, *City Form and Natural Process*, Routledge, 1989
- McHarg, Ian L., *Design with Nature*, John Wiley & Sons, 1995
- Spirn, Anne W., *The Granite Garden: Urban Nature and Human Design*, Basic Books, 1985
- Yeang, Ken, *Designing with Nature: Ecological Basis for Architectural Design*, McGraw-Hill, 1994
  – *Ecodesign: A Manual for Ecological Design*, John Wiley & Sons, 2008
  – *Ecomimicry: Ecological Design By Imitating Ecosystems*, Routledge, 2013

Chapter 3 case studies
- Aphrodite Hill Resort, Cyprus
  http://www.aphroditehillsresortholidays.com/
- Hedeland Arena, nr Roskilde, Denmark
  www.hedeland.dk/
- Waterfront and Market Place, Odda, Norway
  www.blark.no/

Chapter 4 Representing the Landscape Design

Drawing and sketchbooks
- Campanario, Gabriel, *The Art of Urban Sketching: Drawing on Location Around the World*, Quarry Books, 2012
- King, Francis F.D., *Drawing: A Creative Process*, John Wiley & Sons, 1989
- Hutchison, Edward, *Drawing for Landscape Architecture, Sketch to Screen to Site*, Thames & Hudson, 2011
- Reid, Grant, *Landscape Graphics*, Watson-Guptill, 2002
- Sullivan, Chip, *Drawing the Landscape* John Wiley & Sons, 2004

- Wang, Thomas C., *Plan and Section Drawing*, John Wiley & Sons, 1996
  – *Pencil Sketching*, John Wiley & Sons, 2001

- http://gonzogardens.com/
- http://www.urbansketchers.org

3-D modelling and video
- Dunn, Nick, *Architectural Modelmaking*, Laurence King, 2010
- Speranza, Olivia, *The Moviemaking with Your Camera Field Guide: The Essential Guide to Shooting Video with HDSLRs and Digital Cameras*, Ilex, 2012

- Chicago Architecture Today
  http://www.youtube.com/watch?v=47lD_XQ5ID8

Photography
- Farrell, Ian, *A Complete Guide to Digital Photography*, Quercus, 2011
- *Lonely Planet's Guide to Travel Photography*, Lonely Planet Publications, 2012

- http://photo.net/ includes Bob Atkins *Digital Cameras – a Simple Beginner's Guide*, 2003

Digital design
- Bishop, Ian & Lange, Eckhart, *Visualisation in Landscape and Environmental Planning: Technology & Environment*, Taylor & Francis, 2005
- Cantrell, Bradley & Michaels, Wes, *Digital Drawing for Landscape Architecture: Contemporary Techniques and Tools for Digital Representation in Site Design*, John Wiley & Sons, 2010 (raster and vector images and *Adobe Illustrator, Photoshop, and Acrobat*)
- Evening, Martin, *Adobe Photoshop CS5 for Photographers, a Professional Image Editor's Guide to the Creative Use of Photoshop for the Macintosh and PC*, Focal Press, 2010
- Tal, Daniel, *Google SketchUp for Site Design: A Guide to Modeling Site Plans, Terrain and Architecture*, John Wiley & Sons, 2009
- — *Rendering in SketchUp: From Modeling to Presentation for Architecture, Landscape Architecture and Interior Design*, John Wiley & Sons, 2013

- http://www.cadtutor.net/ (AutoCAD, 3ds Max, Photoshop and Bryce)

Building Information Modelling (BIM)
- Crotty, Ray, *The Impact of Building Information Modelling: Transforming Construction*, Routledge, 2011

- http://www.buildingsmart.org/

Mapping, air photography, satellite imagery, GIS
- Corner, James & MacLean, Alex S., *Taking Measures Across the American Landscape*, Yale University Press, 2000
- Cosgrove, Denis, *Mappings*, Reaktion Books, 1999
- Fawcett-Tang, Roger, *Mapping: An Illustrated Guide to Graphic Navigational Systems*, Rotovision, 2005

- The Professional Aerial Photographers Association (PAPA) has a brief useful history and introduction on http://www.papainternational.org/
- NASA websites: a general introduction http://earthobservatory.nasa.gov/
- NASA crew observations http://eol.jsc.nasa.gov
- Specialist NASA collections include the Cities Collection, Volcanoes and Glaciers and one on the Terra satellite, which monitors the Earth's atmosphere, ocean, land, snow and ice, and energy budget http://terra.nasa.gov/
- http://www.esa.int/Our_Activities/Observing_the_Earth

Report writing
- Shaughnessy, Adrian, *Graphic Design: A User's Manual*, Laurence King, 2009
- Williams, Robin, *Non-Designer's Design Book*, Peachpit Press, 2008

- The UK Design Council lists basic introductions to graphic design at http://www.yourcreativefuture.org.uk/graphic_design/graphic10.htm#

Live presentations
- Burden, Ernet, *Design Presentation: Techniques for Marketing and Project Proposals*, McGraw-Hill Inc., 1992
- Reimold, Cheryl & Peter, *The Short Road to Great Presentations: How to Reach Any Audience Through Focussed Preparation, Inspired Delivery, and Smart Use of Technology*, Wiley-Blackwell, 2003
- Weinschenk, Susan, *100 Things Every Designer Needs to Know About People: What Makes Them Tick?*, New Riders, 2012

Chapter 5 From Design Team to Long-term Landscape Management

The stages of work
- The Landscape Institute stages of work are described in *Landscape Institute Engaging a Landscape Consultant, Guidance for Clients on Fees*: 2002 available on
  http://www.landscapeinstitute.org/publications/download/Guidance%20for%20Clients%20on%20Fees.pdf
- RIBA listing of stages is the *Plan of Work* (2007) downloadable from http://www.architecture.com/UseAnArchitect/GuidanceAndPublications/WorkWithAnArchitect.aspx
  http://www.architecture.com/Files/RIBAProfessionalServices/Practice/FrontlineLetters/RIBAPlanofWork2013ConsultationDocument.pdf
- http://www.ribabookshops.com/item/riba-outline-plan-of-work-2007-including-corrigenda-issued-january-2009/100004/

Multi-disciplinary design teams, contracts
- Chappel, David & Willis, Andrew, *Architect in Practice*, Wiley-Blackwell, 2010
- Lupton, Sarah, Cox, Stanley & Clamp, Hugh, *Which Contract?*, RIBA Publishing, 2007

Costing a project
- ASLA has resources on sources of finance for landscape projects, see Economic Models: Project Financing Resources ref. http://www.asla.org/ContentDetail.aspx?id=31832
- Davis Langdon *Spon's External Works and Landscape Price Guide 2013* with similar guides on civil engineering and highways, on mechanical and electrical engineering and on architecture and building. The annual publication is supplemented by quarterly updates available via their website.
- Estimating guides, for estimation in the initial stages of a project, for instance:
  Spain, Bryan, *Spon's Estimating Costs Guide to Small Groundworks, Landscaping and Gardening*, 2007
- The Royal Institute of Chartered Surveyors (RICS) publishes the Building Cost Information Service (BICS) available at http://www.bcis.co.uk/site/scripts/home_info.aspx?homepageID=37
- CABE Space cost studies of parks include *Making the Invisible Visible: the Real Value of Park Assets*, 2009 available at http://webarchive.nationalarchives.gov.uk/20110118095356/http://www.cabe.org.uk/publications/making-the-invisible-visible

Landscape management
- Barber, Alan, *A Guide to Management Plans for Parks and Open Spaces (plus supplement)*, Institute of Leisure and Amenity Management, 1991
- Van Der Zanden, Ann-Marie, *Sustainable Landscape Management: Design, Construction, and Maintenance*, John Wiley & Sons, 2011
- Watkins, John & Wright, Thomas, *The Management and Maintenance of Historic Parks, Gardens and Landscapes: The English Heritage Handbook*, Frances Lincoln, 2007.

- CABE Space *A Guide to Producing Park and Green Space Management Plans*: 2004 http://webarchive.nationalarchives.gov.uk/20110118095356/http://www.cabe.org.uk/publications/producing-parks-and-green-space-management-plans
- A general introduction to cultural landscapes is http://www.english-heritage.org.uk/professional/research/landscapes-and-areas/protected-landscapes/
- The US National Parks Service http://www.nps.gov/history/

Chapter 5 case studies
- London 2012 Olympic Park
  Hopkins, John C. & Neal, Peter, *The Making of the Queen Elizabeth Olympic Park*, John Wiley & Sons, 2012
  Olympic Delivery Authority (the archived website)
  http://www.culture.gov.uk/what_we_do/2012_olympic_games_

and_paralympic_games/6467.aspx
- **The Parks Trust, Milton Keynes, UK**
  www.theparkstrust.com/
- **Dr Jac. P. Thijssepark, Amstelveen, the Netherlands**
  www.thijssepark.nl/

Chapter 6 Education and Employment

Education websites
- An introduction to landscape architecture as a career on the ASLA website: http://www.asla.org/CareerDiscovery.aspx
- Links to a whole series of chatrooms and blogs with public access. http://www.asla.org/sustainablelandscapes/
- Promotion of landscape architecture generally http://www.asla.org/design/
- US schools of landscape architecture http://www.asla.org/Schools.aspx
- Canadian, Australian and New Zealand schools http://www.thecela.org/school-list.php
- The (British) Landscape Institute's website http://www.landscapeinstitute.org/careers/index.php
- http://www.iwanttobealandscapearchitect.com/
- Dutch landscape architecture schools and the professional body http://www.dutchschooloflandscapearchitecture.nl/en/
- Links to other national European associations and their approved landscape architecture programmes http://europe.iflaonline.org/
- European Council of Landscape Schools (ECLAS) http://www.eclas.org/
- A list of national associations worldwide http://www.iflaonline.org/ under Member Associations.

Internships
- http://europe.iflaonline.org/images/PDF/120715_landscape_internshipguide_rh.pdf

Setting up your own business
- Rogers, Walter, *The Professional Practice of Landscape Architecture: A Complete Guide to Starting and Running Your Own Firm,* John Wiley & Sons, 2010

- http://www.architecture-student.com/professional-practice/things-to-do-before-setting-up-practice-in-architecture/

Chapter 6 case studies
- **Thames Landscape Strategy, UK**
  Wilkie, Kim, *Led by the Land: Landscapes by Kim Wilkie,* Frances Lincoln, 2012
  http://www.thames-landscape-strategy.org.uk/
  http://www.londons-arcadia.org.uk/
  http://www.kimwilkie.com/
- **Druk White Lotus School, Ladakh, India**
  The school website: http://www.dwls.org/
  Arup website: http://www.arup.com/Projects/Druk_White_Lotus_School.aspx
  Podcast about the school: http://www.youtube.com/watch?v=fPjaAcvqmpw
  GardenVisit website page on the school with further hyperlinks to blogs and videos: http://www.gardenvisit.com/garden/dragon_garden_dwls_druk_white_lotus_school

Chapter 7 The Future

A changing environment and forecasting
- British Ministry of Defence *Global Strategic Trends out to 2040* http://www.mod.uk/DefenceInternet/MicroSite/DCDC/OurPublications/StrategicTrends+Programme/
- Dynkun, Alexander A. (ed), *Strategic Global Outlook: 2030* Institute for World Economy and International Relations (IMEMO) of the Russian Academy of Sciences: 2011 http://www.imemo.ru/en/publ/2011/forecasts/11001.pdf
- The US National Intelligence Council *Global Trends 2030: An Alternative Future* (2012) available at www.dni.gov/nic/globaltrends

- United Nations Environmental Programme (UNEP) *Global Environment Forecast 5* (2012) http://www.unep.org/geo/geo5.asp
- International Monetary Fund (IMF) databases, include the World Economic Outlook Database available by countries at http://www.imf.org/external/ IMF eLibrary on http://elibrary-data.imf.org/

Some challenges

The environment generally
- US Environmental Protection Agency: http://www.epa.gov/ Urban heat island effect: http://www.epa.gov/heatisld/ Water efficiency: http://www.epa.gov/watersense/outdoor/landscaping_tips.html
- The European Union's European Environment Agency website http://www.eea.europa.eu/ is less a basic introduction and more about policy implementation, e.g. EEA climate change, see http://www.eea.europa.eu/themes

Population growth
- UN world population figures: http://www.un.org/esa/population/ Includes future forecasts. figures on urbanization, and migration.
- United Nations Human Settlements Programme, overview of settlement figures: http://www.unhabitat.org/categories.asp?catid=9
- Regarding unplanned and slums, refer to the film *Dharavi, Slum for Sale* (2010) http://www.imdb.com/title/tt1188984/
- Slum Dwellers International http://www.sdinet.org/
- US-based international think tank: http://www.affordablehousinginstitute.org/
- Largely governmental think tank which argues for slum upgrading: http://www.citiesalliance.org
- User network dealing with city living generally: http://urbz.net/about/
- City think tank with an insight into world-wide ideas about large city management world-wide: http://www.citymayors.com

Climate change
- Helm, Dieter, *The Carbon Crunch: How We're Getting Climate Change Wrong – and How to Fix It,* Yale University Press, 2012
- Kemp, Martin (ed.), *Zero Carbon Britain 2030,* Centre for Alternative Technology, 2010 supplemented by their website http://www.zerocarbonbritain.com/
- Stern, Nicholas, *A Blueprint for a Safer Planet: How to Manage Climate Change and Create a New Era of Progress and Prosperity,* Bodley Head, 2009.
- Sullivan, Chip, *Garden and Climate: Old World Techniques for Landscape Design,* McGraw-Hill, 2002

- *Stern Review on the Economics of Climate Change*, H.M. Treasury, 2006 was a study of climate change by the British economist Nicholas Stern, available in 12 languages apart from English and online at http://webarchive.nationalarchives.gov.uk/+/http://www.hm-treasury.gov.uk/independent_reviews/stern_review_economics_climate_change/stern_review_report.cfm
- The Landscape Institute position statement is *Landscape Architecture and the Challenge of Climate Change*: 2008 and is downloadable from their website from http://www.landscapeinstitute.org/policy/ClimateChange.php
- The ASLA web page on climate change has links to many other websites and resources: http://www.asla.org/climatechange.aspx

Resources and raw materials, sustainability, recycling and everyday practice
- Berge, Bjørn, *The Ecology of Building Materials,* Architectural Press, 2009
- Holden, Robert & Liversedge, Jamie, *Construction for Landscape Architecture,* Laurence King, 2012
- Thompson, J. William & Sorvig, Kim, *Sustainable Landscape Construction: A Guide to Green Building Outdoors,* Island Press, 2008

- The ASLA sustainability toolkit places such sustainability ideas in a wider context, see http://www.asla.org/ContentDetail.aspx?id=26992

Air:
- Calthorpe, Peter, *Urbanism in the Age of Climate Change,* Island Press, 2011
- Gehl, Jan, *Life Between Buildings, Using Public Space,* Island Press, 2011
- Lombardi, D. Rachel, Leach, Joanne & Rogers, Chris, *Designing Resilient Cities: A Guide to Good Practice,* IHS BRE Press, 2012

- Armour, Tom, Job, Mark & Canavan, Rory *The Benefits of Large Species Trees in Urban Landscapes: a Costing, Design and Management Guide* C712 CIRIA: 2012 available at http://www.ciria.org/service/Web_Site/AM/ContentManagerNet/ContentDisplay.aspx?Section=Web_Site&ContentID=22853 link doesn't work
- British Urban Futures research project https://connect.innovateuk.org/web/urban-futures

Water
- Dreiseitl, Herbert, *Recent Waterscapes: Planning, Building and Designing with Water,* Birkhäuser GmbH, 2009

- Dutch State *National Water Plan 2009* http://english.verkeerenwaterstaat.nl/english/topics/water/water_and_the_future/national_water_plan/
- The English Environment Agency website http://www.environment-agency.gov.uk/ has flood maps and publications and case studies on coastal retreat (aka managed retreat).
- US Department of Agriculture, National Water Program, http://www.usawaterquality.org/themes/watershed/research/default.html
- The Construction Industry Research and Information Association (www.ciria.org) publishes practical guides on issues such as SUDS (sustainable drainage systems) http://www.ciria.org/service/content_by_themes/AM/ContentManagerNet/Default.aspx?Section=content_by_themes&Template=/TaggedPage/TaggedPageDisplay.cfm&TPLID=19&ContentID=10559

Energy
- Glasson, John, Therivel, Riki, & Chadwick, Andrew, A., *Introduction to Environmental Impact Assessment,* Routledge, 2011
- Landscape Institute & Institute of Environmental Management and Assessment, *Guidelines for Landscape and Visual Impact Assessment,* Taylor & Francis, 2002
- MacKay, David J.C., *Sustainable Energy – Without the Hot Air,* UIT, 2009

- For an introduction to what current energy thinking involves for landscape planning scale refer to the Scottish Government site http://www.snh.gov.uk/protecting-scotlands-nature/looking-after-landscapes/landscape-policy-and-guidance/landscape-planning-and-development/landscape-and-energy/

Food and greening
- Warren, John, Lawson, Clare & Belcher, Kenneth, *The Agri-Environment: Theory and Practice of Managing the Environmental Impacts of Agriculture,* Cambridge University Press, 2007
- Westmacott, Richard & Worthington, Tom, *Agricultural Landscapes: A Third Look,* Countryside Agency, 1997

- The Desert Restoration Hub initiated by Greenwich-based landscape architect, Dr Benz Kotzen, addresses the issues of arid lands and combating desertification http://desertrestorationhub.com/
- For a world-wide overview refer to the UN Food and Agriculture Organisation http://www.fao.org/index_en.htm

- One area where landscape architects have taken an interest, is the relatively passive process of Landscape Character Assessment and the UK government agency Natural England has a useful webpage on this at http://www.naturalengland.org.uk/ourwork/landscape/englands/character/assessment/default.aspx where one can download the Countryside Agency and Scottish Natural Heritage *Landscape Character Assessment Guidance, Guidance for England and Wales*: 2002.
- There has, however, been much more interest among landscape architecture in urban agriculture for instance the ASLA introduction *The Edible City* http://www.asla.org/sustainablelandscapes/Vid_UrbanAg.html
- There is a page on urban forestry on the ASLA website http://www.asla.org/sustainablelandscapes/Vid_UrbanForests.html

Biodiversity
- http://www.wwf.org/ http://wwf.panda.org/about_our_earth/all_publications/living_planet_report/
- http://www.oneplanetliving.org/index.html
- The International Union for the Conservation of Nature (IUCN) offers conservation databases and action tools. http://www.iucn.org/
- Most countries have their own specialist agencies and NGOs as well, such as: Natural England http://www.naturalengland.org.uk/ US Nature Conservancy http://www.nature.org/

Chapter 7 case studies
- **Dutch National Water Plan** http://english.verkeerenwaterstaat.nl/english/topics/water/water_and_the_future/national_water_plan/ This study was initiated by the Delta Commission of 2007–8 set up to report on the impact of sea level rise, so it is worth reviewing its advice http://www.deltacommissie.com/en/advies
- **Downing Roads Mooring, Shad Thames, London, UK** http://www.savethemoorings.org.uk/ Elaine Hughes's own website is http://elainehughes.co.uk/?page_id=647
- **Korail, Dhaka, Banglasdesh** The Bangladeshi television ATN news report on the work of landscape architect Khondaker Hasibul Kabir in the Korail http://www.youtube.com/watch?v=YM7eSOJLJ1g Alex Davies *Creating Public Green Space on a Lake in One of the World's Densest Slums,* 2012 at http://www.treehugger.com/urban-design/community-garden-lake-bangladesh-improves-slum.html
- **North Holland Coastline Study, the Netherlands** http://www.arcadis.com/index.aspx http://www.arcadis.nl/Pers/publicaties/Documents/10-1710%20Flood%20protection%20and%20risk%20management%20low%20res.pdf Giardino, Alessio, Santinelli, Giorgio & Bruens, Ankie *The State of the Coast (Toestand van de kust) Case Study: North Holland,* Deltares, 2012 1206171-003 at http://repository.tudelft.nl:8888/recordview/view?recordId=HYDRO%3Aoai%3Atudelft.nl%3Auuid%3A74695605-a373-4667-8942-796251e955d7&language=en

The World Wide Web changes and websites go out of use. You may find some websites that are no longer directly accessible by looking on the Wayback Archive http://web.archive.org/

A longer version of this bibliography appears online.

Index

Picture Credits

Apart from those images listed below, all photographs are by the authors; all line drawings are by Jamie Liversedge.

8a Mary Hooper; 11d Crown Copyright http://goc2012.culture.gov.uk/flickr/olympic-park-aerial-photo/ re-use of this information resource should be sent to e-mail:psi@nationalarchives.gsi.gov.uk; 11e Aero Camera Hofmeester; 13b D.Paysage; 17b Paddy Clarke; 22a British Library/Robana via Getty Images; 25a Paddy Clarke; 26a Frances Benjamin Johnson Collection, Library of Congress. source http://www.loc.gov/pictures/item/92501035/; 27b Courtesy of the Westchester County Archives; 27c Library of Congress, Prints & Photographs Division, FSA/OWI Collection, reproduction no. LC-USF34-072401-D; 32b Thinkstock; 33b National Park Service; 35b Région Ile-de-France; 35c Cornwall Council; 36a RIBA Library Photographs Collection; 38a Getty Images; 39c Room 4.1.3; 40b OMA/ Architecture d'Aujourhui; 41D Paddy Clarke; 41e Mary Hooper; 41f Mary Hooper; 41g Paddy Clarke; 41h Mary Hooper; 42a West 8 Urban Design & Landscape Architecture; 42b West 8 Urban Design & Landscape Architecture; 42c Municipality of Madrid; 53a and b David Watson; 55a NASA; 55b NASA; 55c NASA; 55d Istock/cgnznt144; 55e Ministerie van Verkeer en Waterstaat, Rijksdienst voor de IJsselmeerpolders; 64a Mary Hooper; 67b Gustafson Porter; 70a Paddy Clarke; 71b Mary Hooper; 71c–e Paddy Clarke; 87f Lanitis Development Ltd.; 90c The Centurion Club Ltd., St.Albans; 91a Bernard Tschumi; 92b and c Marian Boswall; 93g Clouston; 99c Christopher C. Benson/ KAP Cris; 108–09 All images Bjorbekk & Lindheim AS Landscape Architects; 117 All images Gollifer Langston Architects; 122 Both images David Watson; 125 European Space Agency, Galileo; 126 All images Shelley Mosco; 127 Both images David Watson; 135 D. Paysage; 136a Paddy Clarke; 137b and c Peter Neale; 137d Sue Willmott; 137e London Legacy Development Corporation; 145b Grant Associates; 146c Grant Associates; 165 Olin/ Sahar Coston-Hardy; 167 All images Kim Wilkie; 171 All images Simon Drury Brown; 172 NASA Earth Observation mission 30 satellite crew photograph; 177 Istock (photographer Joseph Nickischer); 178–79 All images Dutch Ministry of Infrastructure and Environment (Ministerie van Infrastructuur en Milieu); 186–87 All images Khondaker Hasibul Kabir; 190–91 Arcadis/ Hoogheemraadschap Hollands Noorderkwartier/ beeldbank.rws.nl Rijkswaterstaat, the Netherlands.

Jacket image: High Line Park, Manhattan, © Cameron Davidson/Corbis

Acknowledgements

The authors acknowledge the patient support, and help and of our main editor, Peter Jones; our initial editor Liz Faber; our book designer Michael Lenz; and Philip Cooper, editorial director at Laurence King, who commissioned us.

This book is dedicated to the Landscape Architecture students at the University of Greenwich who have inspired and provoked us over three decades.